The *Leadership in Action* Series

ON LEADING IN TIMES OF CHANGE

Center for
Creative
Leadership

www.ccl.org

The Center for Creative Leadership is an international, nonprofit educational institution founded in 1970 to advance the understanding, practice, and development of leadership for the benefit of society worldwide. As a part of this mission, it publishes books and reports that aim to contribute to a general process of inquiry and understanding in which ideas related to leadership are raised, exchanged, and evaluated. The ideas presented in its publications are those of the author or authors.

The Center thanks you for supporting its work through the purchase of this volume. If you have comments, suggestions, or questions about any CCL Press publications, please contact the Director of Publications at the address given below.

Center for Creative Leadership
Post Office Box 26300
Greensboro, North Carolina 27438-6300
Telephone 336 288 7210
www.ccl.org

Stephen Rush, Editor

With an Introduction by Kerry A. Bunker

The *Leadership in Action* Series

ON LEADING IN TIMES OF CHANGE

CENTER FOR CREATIVE LEADERSHIP

Greensboro, North Carolina

CCL Stock Number 196
©2012 Center for Creative Leadership

Published by CCL Press
Sylvester Taylor, Director of Assessments, Tools, and Publications
Peter Scisco, Manager, Publication Development
Stephen Rush, Editor
Karen Lewis, Editor

Design and layout by Joanne Ferguson

Library of Congress Cataloging-in-Publication Data

On leading in times of change / Stephen Rush, editor ; with an introduction by Kerry A. Bunker.
    p. cm. — (The leadership in action series)
  Includes bibliographical references and index.
  ISBN 978-1-60491-120-6 (print on demand : alk. paper) — ISBN 978-1-60491-121-3 (e-book) 1. Leadership. 2. Executive ability. 3. Organizational change. I. Rush, Stephen, 1954-

  HD57.7.O47 2012
  658.4'092—dc23

                                                        2012007854

CONTENTS

INTRODUCTION

Many years ago, when I was a young, wide-eyed organizational psychologist, a wise mentor gave me sage advice on understanding the psychology of human behavior. He said: "All of psychology is essentially the understanding of learning. If people have the ability to learn, everything else takes care of itself." His wisdom seems particularly appropriate for understanding the challenges of leading in our modern world. We live in a time when the notions of evolutionary or incremental change seem as much a relic of history as the Walkman and the typewriter. Gone are the days of sequential and predictable change with clear outcome goals, a rational window for implementation, and easily identifiable action steps to guide the journey. Gone as well are the safety nets and lifelines that allowed an easy return to the comfortable and familiar strategies of the past if we somehow ventured down the wrong path in our quest for something new, exciting, or more productive. Today, the ability to learn is key. We find ourselves confronting wave upon wave of tumultuous and unanticipated change events, each one demanding rapid learning, resilient adaptability, and enormous leaps of faith and commitment.

The good news about living and leading in what the U.S. Army War College has termed a VUCA (volatility, uncertainty, complexity, and ambiguity) world is that it regularly presents the necessary *challenge* to trigger needed learning and growth. But the power of this challenge can be wasted if the goal lies beyond the reach of the target audience or if leaders fail to accurately *assess* where people are in terms of their emotional reaction and their capacity for undertaking new learning. Success can also be undermined by a failure to offer timely and authentic *support* along the way. Change events can be powerful opportunities to learn—but only if all the ingredients of development are blended into the experience in sufficient amounts, at appropriate times, and with genuine compassion and sensitivity. A challenging and provocative change agenda that is supported with guidance and understanding can actually lay the foundation for helping individuals and organizations learn to thrive in the face of future challenges. It works like this: leading people through a challenging learning experience builds character and resiliency, which in turn enhances confidence to take on new challenges, which then opens the door to new experiences and creates greater readiness for inviting new learning opportunities.

This fieldbook is intended to help you explore diverse perspectives on leading yourself, others, and your organization through times of complex and relentless change and uncertainty. You're going to hear many different voices in the content that follows, but there are common threads in terms of self-awareness, vulnerability and openness, adaptability, managing paradox, emotional intelligence, and leading with authenticity. Underlying it all is the core capacity of *learning how to learn*. This book is drawn from articles published in CCL's magazine, *Leadership in Action*, between 2000 and 2010 and is the second in a series covering topics such as Filling the Leadership Pipeline, Innovation and Creativity, Leading Globally, and more. Following are some of the perspectives shared in this volume:

Gary Yukl and Richard Lepsinger provide an overall framework for understanding leadership in the context of change and offer guided steps for making it happen. Kerry A. Bunker and Michael Wakefield focus the lens specifically on leading with authenticity in times of transition, with a specific emphasis on managing the paradoxical demands of both creating and implementing the change *and* understanding and supporting people through the emotional discomfort of learning. Gene Klann provides a concrete example of implementing a large-scale version of this paradoxical process in the post-Vietnam War reconfiguration of the U.S. Army.

Another cluster of articles focuses on the "inside-out" nature of leading in a VUCA world. Continual learning is essential, and self-awareness is a core competency. Robert Goldberg speaks to the importance of leading yourself as a prerequisite to leading others and offers three critical steps for avoiding the traps that frequently derail efforts to implement change. Stu Kantor, Kathy E. Kram, and Fabio Sala make the case for executive adaptability and delineate a quadrant model of change leadership that leverages one's capacity for courage and curiosity—attributes that can be both learned and enhanced through experience. Similarly, Christopher Musselwhite makes the case for understanding one's own comfort zone and preferred style of responding to change. He demonstrates how each response style adds unique value in times of change and offers a framework for identifying and leveraging the preferences of others.

There is general agreement that adaptability and learning are critical elements of living and learning in times of change. A number of the articles offer insights and guidance for nurturing these attributes in oneself and others. Paige Graham and Allan Calarco present a well-researched model for understanding the essence of adaptability, and Calarco and Joan Gurvis outline the steps and process for enhancing adaptability in yourself and others.

A number of the authors speak to the notion that potent learning is hard work and always involves a mix of positive and negative emotions. Leaders who fail to understand the short-term decrement in performance that comes with letting go of past learning to acquire the new will not be successful in leading themselves or others through times of change. Keir Carroll advocates for seeing *the luxury of tough times* and suggests five terrific questions to enhance reflection, learning, and insight in difficult leadership situations. His article addresses one of the fundamental challenges of leadership—making time to step outside yourself and learn from experience at the very moments that you are under the most pressure to perform—or even to survive. Similarly, Graham Jones describes how change leaders must find comfort in being simultaneously strong and vulnerable in order to both drive change and be patient with followers. His distinction between *safe leaders* and *real leaders* speaks directly to the challenge of learning and leading in times of change.

Another cluster of articles is directly focused on tools and processes for nurturing and supporting adaptability and learning in others. Bunker provides a leader's guide for assessing the capacity and comfort of others in responding to the unfolding demands of a VUCA world and offers a framework and toolkit for helping individuals be more successful in responding to the changes they face. Meena Wilson and Susan Rice discuss research that stresses the importance of inspirational leadership and outlines a process to help leaders develop people who are more adaptable, more resilient, and more likely to sustain learning in a turbulent environment. Klann again provides a real-world example as he describes the core elements utilized to reestablish and crystalize leadership in the wake of major crisis events such as 9/11 and the national financial calamity.

A final thread that emerges from the entire volume involves the importance of understanding a person's, organization's, or even culture's *story* in leading through change. At the individual level, each of us is unique, with our own pattern of culture, personality, and perhaps most importantly, experience. As human beings we learn through the process of story—both our own and those of others. Nick Nessley and Stedman Graham speak directly to the power of the *narrative lens* in guiding others through adverse times. Rescripting one's own story and sharing it with others lies at the heart of both authenticity and leading change. At the organizational level, Nick Yacabucci emphasizes the importance of connecting with employees directly during downsizing or restructuring as a means of helping them navigate through their own situation so that they can turn a potentially painful process into a more controllable and positive experience. Finally, Yi Zhang presents recent research demonstrating how three countries in varying stages of evolution and change tend to focus on different aspects of the experiences they encounter and emerge with different lessons for the future.

I encourage you to dive into these articles and craft your own pathway for learning to lead yourself and others through the complexity and challenge of our VUCA world. The answers are not simple but the authors have shared a wealth of insight to get you started and guide you on the journey. Enjoy!

Kerry A. Bunker, Ph.D.
Founder and President, Mangrove Leadership Solutions
Founding Partner, MEM Partners (Making Experience Matter)
Senior Fellow, Human Capital at The Conference Board

Leading Change: Adapting and Innovating in an Uncertain World

Gary Yukl and Richard Lepsinger

In today's turbulent business environment, being able to respond in a timely way to emerging threats and opportunities is crucial to an organization's survival and prosperity. An organization's effectiveness can be improved by leader decisions that facilitate innovation and adaptation.

Why do some companies consistently outperform their peers? It could be an innovative business strategy, a unique business model, favorable economic conditions, or any of a number of other factors. But when companies that face identical circumstances are compared, one variable stands out among the winners—leadership quality. The best leaders are able to effectively influence three determinants of organizational performance—adaptation, efficiency, and human resources. In this article we will focus on adaptation.

Adaptation involves changes made to cope with external threats and to exploit opportunities created by new technology, changing markets, and the shifting needs and expectations of customers.

The ability to adapt becomes even more important when the external environment is turbulent and uncertain. Uncertainty is greater in times of rapid technological change, political and economic turmoil, or new threats from competitors. In these situations, innovation is usually necessary to develop an appropriate response to emerging threats and opportunities. Examples of organizations that face uncertain environments include telecommunications and computer products companies, research laboratories, military combat units, and companies in recently deregulated industries, such as financial services and energy utilities.

Another condition that increases the importance of adaptation is a competitive strategy that emphasizes unique, leading-edge products or services. For such a strategy to be effective there must be frequent innovation and rapid response to threats and opportunities. Examples of industries in which organizations need to be very responsive to changing customer preferences, new technology, and new initiatives by competitors include fashion clothing, pharmaceuticals, medical equipment, computer products, advertising, and entertainment.

HOW TO LEAD CHANGE

The many difficulties involved in fostering adaptation in large organizations make it essential to have a culture with firmly embedded values and beliefs that support innovation and change. Relevant values include flexibility, continuous improvement, initiative, and a quest for excellence. Instead of viewing adaptation

as an infrequent reaction to dramatic, onetime events, it is better to view it as a continuous process that involves a combination of many and frequent incremental improvements and occasional major changes. In organizations with this type of culture, new ideas are nurtured and promoted, information is widely and freely shared, and people and systems are flexible and ready to respond to changes when they occur. Over an extended period of time the leaders of an organization can strengthen cultural values that encourage innovation and flexibility.

In addition to applying their influence on organizational culture, leaders can use specific behaviors and take specific actions to facilitate innovation and adaptation.

Monitoring the Environment

Monitoring the environment involves collecting and analyzing information about opportunities and threats in the external environment and identifying trends and opportunities to enhance business performance. The focus of external monitoring should be the sectors of the environment on which the work unit is highly dependent (such as clients and customers, suppliers, competitors, or governmental agencies).

External monitoring is often assumed to be the province of senior leaders, but it is the people in direct contact with customers, such as sales and service representatives, who often first get wind of changes in customer needs or competitor actions. Thus environmental scanning and interpretation of events should not be left entirely to the CEO and other top executives. External monitoring in organizations is more effective when people at all levels are involved and relevant information is recognized and used to improve strategic decisions.

Strategic Planning

Strategic planning is the process of determining where you are, where you want to be in the future, and how you will get from here to there. The process includes setting strategic objectives, identifying tactics and actions for attaining them, and determining the resources and actions needed to implement the strategies. Although senior management has the ultimate responsibility for strategic decisions, the most successful leaders find ways to involve people throughout the organization in the strategic planning process.

A strategy will not improve organizational performance unless it is relevant and feasible. The likelihood that an organization will be able to achieve a competitive advantage is determined, in part, by its ability to identify and leverage its core competencies— its knowledge about particular activities and its ability to carry out those activities. Core competencies can be the key to the future success of an organization; they help it remain competitive in its current business and enable it to diversify into new businesses.

Envisioning Change

Painting a vivid, appealing picture of what your organization wants to accomplish or become helps to communicate the desired outcomes of a change initiative in a way that is understandable, meaningful, and inspiring. Envisioning change is about putting opportunities and threats in context and clarifying how the organization needs to respond. A variety of elements may be included in the vision, such as strategic objectives, key values for the company, general approaches for attaining the vision, slogans and symbols, and a description of what the vision will mean to people when it is attained.

In times of great change, people look to their leaders for direction and signs that the organization has selected the right course of action. Therefore it is essential to communicate personal confidence that the vision can be achieved and that the benefits will be worth the short-term sacrifices. Leaders can convey a message of confidence and optimism through the type of language they use and by consistent actions that demonstrate their conviction and support of the vision.

Building Support for Change

Although most people would agree that change is essential if an organization is to adapt, grow, and remain competitive, change often produces anxiety and resistance. For people to support change, they must see it as necessary and feasible. Leaders can build such support by explaining the urgent need for change, building a broad coalition of supporters, identifying likely opponents and reasons for their resistance, and taking action to deal with resistance.

The complex task of persuading people to support major change in an organization is too big a job for a single leader. It is essential to build a coalition of supporters inside and outside the organization. These external members could include labor union leaders, important clients, government officials, or executives of financial institutions. To succeed in gaining the approval and support of a proposed change from key people, a leader needs to understand how people feel about the change and whether they are likely to be supporters or opponents.

Implementing Change

It is impossible to anticipate all the potential problems created by a major change or to prepare detailed plans for carrying out every aspect of the change. A change program is less likely to be successful if a top-level leader tries to dictate in detail how it will be implemented in each part of the organization. Authority to make decisions and deal with problems should be delegated to the leaders who are responsible for implementing change in their subunits.

After the process of change is under way, the primary leadership roles for top management are to provide encouragement, support, and necessary resources to those leaders who are serving as change agents, and to guide and coordinate change efforts across different subunits of the organization. Leadership behaviors that facilitate implementation of change include filling key positions with competent change agents, preparing people to adjust to change and cope with the pain of making a transition, providing opportunities to celebrate early successes, keeping people informed about the progress of the change, and ensuring that leaders demonstrate continued commitment to the change.

Although responsibility for guiding various aspects of the change can be delegated to additional change agents, the leader who is identified as the primary proponent or sponsor of the change must continue to provide the attention and endorsement that signal a commitment to seeing the change through to the end.

Encouraging Innovative Thinking

Identifying innovative ways to improve strategies, processes, products, or services is one requirement for successful adaptation, and there are many ways a leader can promote more innovative thinking by employees. The leader can encourage people to look at problems from multiple perspectives, to question implicit assumptions about the work, and to brainstorm better ways to do things. Another approach for encouraging innovative thinking is to set innovation goals for units or individuals. When there is a specific innovation goal for which people will be held accountable, this mental activity is more likely to get the attention and effort it deserves.

Innovative thinking is also increased by getting people to look at problems from a different perspective. For example, engineers have been trying for years to improve the battery life of laptop computers by focusing on longer-lasting batteries and software solutions that dim or shut off the display. The engineers at 3M's Microreplication Technology Center reframed the problem— by asking how they could make a display that used less power. With this frame of reference they turned to a technology used in the 1950s to increase the brightness of overhead projectors and adapted it to magnify the brightness of backlit flat-panel displays. Their *brightness enhancement film* significantly extends battery life and is now being used by numerous laptop manufacturers.

Facilitating Collective Learning

It is important for leaders to create an appreciation for flexibility and learning among people at all levels of the organization. Major change will be more acceptable and less disruptive once people develop pride and confidence in their capacity to adapt and learn. To encourage an appreciation for learning, all practices should be considered temporary and examined regularly to see if they can be improved or eliminated. Leaders should also encourage people to use learning practices such as after-action reviews (also called after-activity reviews or postmortems), experiments, and benchmarking against other organizations.

Leaders also need to encourage an active sharing of ideas and new knowledge in the organization. To maximize the benefits, new knowledge should be widely diffused and applied in the organization. Secrecy is the enemy of learning, whereas easy access to information about the organization's operations—including problems and failures—facilitates learning. Leaders should encourage employees who are facing difficult problems to reach out to other people in the organization to find out how they might have handled similar challenges in the past.

When innovations are developed in one part of the organization, leaders can facilitate diffusion of this knowledge to other parts of the organization in several ways. After an innovative change has been implemented successfully in one unit, some members of that unit can be transferred to other units to help implement the same type of change. Seminars and workshops can be conducted by internal experts or outside consultants to teach people how to perform new activities or use new technology. When it is not feasible for people to attend formal training, a team of experts can be dispatched to different sites to demonstrate how to use new procedures. Video and Internet-based conferencing capabilities can also be used to promote broad idea sharing in a cost- and time-efficient manner.

BUILDING SYNERGY

The leadership behaviors and actions that facilitate adaptation should be used together in a consistent way to enhance their positive effects and to avoid adverse side effects. For example, monitoring the environment, envisioning change, and strategic planning are frequently used as a set of interrelated leadership behaviors. The discovery of emerging problems or opportunities as a result of external monitoring is of little consequence unless you plan how to deal with them. By applying information gathered from external monitoring, leaders can develop or alter strategic plans to help make the envisioned change a reality. Likewise, monitoring the environment and strategic planning provide much of the context that drives innovation.

Also closely linked are behaviors such as envisioning change, building support for change, and implementing change. It is not enough to explain the need for change or to articulate an appealing vision. To be successful, leaders must build broad support for a proposed change, then guide the processes required to implement the change, which often takes several years of concerted effort.

PROGRAMS AND SYSTEMS

Leaders also use programs, management systems, and structural features to determine what types of changes are desirable and to facilitate innovation and collective learning:

Intrapreneurship programs. New ideas are fragile and do not have a long life expectancy once exposed to a hostile environment (one featuring, for example, the "not invented here" syndrome, a lack of resources and support, or bureaucratic red tape). An intrapreneurship program provides an opportunity to develop new ideas to the point where they can be fairly evaluated.

External benchmarking. Benchmarking is the process of measuring one's own products, services, and practices against those of competitors and companies recognized as industry leaders. By establishing systematic processes of searching for and importing best practices and innovative ideas, a firm can identify ways to improve products, services, and processes.

Understanding customers. Successful adaptation requires a good understanding of customer and client needs and expectations. Knowledge about the attitudes, values, needs, and perceptions of current and potential customers can be used to determine how the company's products or services can be made more appealing. Many companies use market survey techniques, customer panels, and focus groups to assess the reactions of current customers or the preferences of potential customers.

Reward and recognition programs. Many companies use formal programs to identify and recognize innovation by individuals and teams. The successful application of innovative ideas can be showcased through internal media and at special innovation-themed conferences. It is also important to recognize successful efforts to improve sales and customer service, even if no major innovation was involved. Some companies use special ceremonies to celebrate major successes and emphasize the importance of sales and service.

Collective learning practices. Two examples of practices used to discover new knowledge and learn from experience are after-action reviews and controlled experiments. After-action reviews are an effective way to learn from important, recurring initiatives and projects. Members of the organization who participate in the project meet to review what was done correctly, what mistakes were made, and what can be done better next time.

Controlled experiments make it possible to evaluate innovative processes or procedures to assess their consequences and determine how well they work. The amount of learning that results from an experiment depends on how well it is designed and executed. Even a simple experiment can provide useful information.

Knowledge management programs. Some organizations are successful at discovering new knowledge but fail to use it effectively.

Knowledge management systems are used to ensure that new knowledge and learning is retained and disseminated to people who need it in different parts of the organization. Knowledge management is the process of taking information and putting it into a format that can be reused for future work, as well as reviewing the information later to determine how it needs to be changed so it can continue to be useful. These systems also serve as places to store ideas that are a bit ahead of their time but may be useful later or for a purpose other than initially intended.

Structural forms. How the work is structured and the physical proximity of team members can dramatically influence the opportunities people have to discuss ideas and exchange information. Innovative activities such as new product development can also be facilitated by the use of temporary structural arrangements such as cross-functional teams, which include representatives from each functional subunit involved in the project and in some cases representatives from suppliers, clients, and joint-venture partners. Cross-functional teams allow flexible, rapid deployment of personnel and resources to solve problems as they are discovered and help members learn to view a problem or challenge from various perspectives rather than from a single functional viewpoint.

PUTTING IT TOGETHER

Rapid adaptation is relatively more important when the external environment is turbulent and uncertain and when the organization's strategy emphasizes unique, leading-edge products and services. Adaptation may require small incremental improvements or major changes in products, services, operational processes, and the organization's competitive strategy.

Effective leaders assess the external environment to identify threats and opportunities. They help people interpret events and determine the implications for the organization. Such leaders recognize when major change is needed and know how to develop support from the people who can make change happen. Because many innovations in large organizations result from a bottom-up process, effective leaders understand how important it is to inspire and empower all members of the organization to learn from experience, develop creative ideas, and share new knowledge across subunit boundaries. They understand that implementation of major change is a slow and difficult process that requires their consistent attention to succeed. And they use programs, systems, and structural arrangements that are designed to encourage and facilitate innovation and collective learning.

Adaptability: What It Takes to Be a Quick-Change Artist

Paige Graham and Allan Calarco

In today's business world, change is coming faster and bigger than ever before. Companies and even entire industries can find themselves turned upside down seemingly overnight. The need for leaders to be adaptable is generally acknowledged, but there has been little insight into what adaptability actually looks like. Now CCL and two partners are undertaking research to deepen the understanding of adaptability.

*M*etathesiophobia. That's the tongue-tying word for the *fear of change*—a fear that most people, if they are honest with themselves, will admit to having experienced. Change, even when it's relatively minor and even when the individual wants a change, can be unsettling and unnerving—and as a result intimidating. And with fear usually come stress and resistance.

For leaders, fearing and resisting change and balking at venturing into the unknown can be their own, their followers', and their organizations' undoing. It's a truism of today's business environment that the only thing that remains the same is change—and change is more copious, rapid, and complex than ever before. Mergers and acquisitions, corporate restructurings, downsizings, increasing globalization, and market upheavals are just a few of the dramatic transitions that leaders and their organizations must deal with at an unprecedented level. Another source of transition is the ephemerality of technology, with increasingly rapid rates of obsolescence and replacement requiring individuals and organizations to engage in a constant learning process. In addition, the people who make up organizations, work groups, and teams often shift at a breakneck pace. Institutional loyalty is hardly what it used to be (the Bureau of National Affairs recently reported that employee turnover is occurring at the highest rate in nearly twenty years), and it's common for people in organizations to be quickly shuttled in and out of different assignments. Managers' ability to deal with this type of change—losing well-known team members and working with new and unfamiliar

colleagues—has a profound impact on organizational effectiveness and productivity.

FEELING THE HEAT

Statistics bear out the prevalence, increasing scope, and sometimes devastating effects of change in the business world. Of the one hundred largest U.S. companies at the beginning of the twentieth century, only sixteen exist today. And according to government figures, in the past decade in the United States more than 450,000 companies went under, more than 24 million jobs were lost, nearly half of all companies were restructured, more than 80,000 firms were acquired or merged, and more than 700,000 organizations sought bankruptcy protection.

Leaders are well aware of how important change—and the way they and their colleagues react to change—has become to their effectiveness and the success of their organizations. In a recent survey conducted by Ernst & Young and Cap Gemini Ernst & Young, eighty-six executives identified the top three threats that they and their organizations will face in the next two years. The executives cited regulatory changes (38 percent), competitive dynamics (29 percent), and market uncertainty (19 percent). All these concerns are related to transition.

Managers who participate in CCL's The Looking Glass Experience leadership development program indicate that change is omnipresent in today's organizations. Most of these managers say they have been through not just one but multiple acquisitions, mergers, reorganizations, or other significant organizational changes during their careers. They indicate that the pace and degree of change continue to spiral upward.

But recognizing that change inevitably exists is not the same as dealing with it effectively. Even though organizations rise or fall based largely on their ability to react to, manage, control, and introduce change, many managers have little or no understanding of or training in navigating the process of change.

Research conducted by CCL has identified ten flaws that can contribute to derailment—that is, to a manager who has previously been seen as successful and full of potential for continued advancement instead being fired, demoted, or held on a career plateau. Of these ten flaws, *the inability to develop or adapt* was the most frequently cited reason for derailment among North American managers. Conversely, the most frequently cited success factor for North American managers was *the ability to develop or adapt*.

If leaders don't consider their own adaptability and the adaptability of their subordinates, new initiatives can be halted or stifled before they are given a chance, or simply left to die on the vine. When a fresh vision emanates from an organization's top leadership, for instance, managers and their teams are expected to embrace the vision and move it toward implementation as quickly as possible. To understand and get on board with the new vision and to inspire subordinates to do the same, managers need to be adaptable.

During times of change and uncertainty, adaptability is required to foster progress and to help the organization and its members remain effective and productive. It's not enough for leaders to be adaptable themselves, however; they also must be able to recognize adaptability in their employees. This skill helps leaders choose people who are most suited to doing work involving change and who can motivate and act as role models for others during the transition period that accompanies any new initiative.

So it's clear that adaptability is crucial to leaders' effectiveness and success. This probably doesn't strike you as revelatory news. (After all, the subject of change is prominent on many people's radar screens; Spencer Johnson's book *Who Moved My Cheese?*—about the inevitability of change and the need to adapt to the unexpected—is the top-selling business book of all time.) Yet even though the importance of adaptability in leaders is now widely regarded as a given, not much is known about what adaptability actually *looks like*. Until now, little research has been done on the specific behaviors that constitute adaptability. If leaders can gain insight into what these behaviors are, it will help them not only recognize but also take the first steps toward developing adaptability in themselves and others.

UNDER THE MICROSCOPE

To clarify what it means to be adaptable, and to describe what adaptability looks like, CCL has conducted research in collaboration with George Mason University and the U.S. Army. *Adaptability* is a term that is thrown around a lot without a concrete definition or understanding of what it is. By explicitly identifying and describing the behaviors that make up adaptability, the research should help leaders approach adaptability in a more practical way and provide a foundation for recognizing and developing the skill in themselves and others.

The study has focused on three main components of adaptability: cognitive, dispositional (personality related), and emotional. Following is a look at the behaviors that signify proficiency in each adaptive component.

Cognitive

Adaptability requires effective interpretation of change, and the first step is acknowledging that change has occurred. Successful adapters then address key aspects of the change—for example, how a new vision will create new markets, competitors, and organizational roles. Identifying how the change will affect the way the organization functions is also important.

The ability to formulate alternative strategies is another aspect of cognitive adaptability. Leaders who are adaptable are able to let go of old roles and ideas, identify and embrace new roles, and come up with new tactics and action plans that address the implications of the change. Specifically, their language often shifts from past tense ("We used to do this . . .") to future tense ("Now we will do this . . .").

Cognitive adaptability also involves divergent thinking—for instance, contemplating a totally new direction that turns the change into an advantage, or acknowledging and putting to use the skills of new members of a team. Finally, cognitive adapters are good at spanning boundaries—they consider the implications of the change for others in the organization and communicate this information to the various organizational units and top management.

Dispositional

The ability to remain optimistic—but at the same time realistic—is one of the linchpins of adaptability. Successful adapters approach change not as a threat but as an opportunity. They take the attitude that they can continue to be effective in the new environment. Optimism also appears to boost managers' self-confidence in their ability to be effective during times of change.

It's debatable whether optimism can be developed, but next time you are in a situation of change, try identifying something that is positive about the situation and building on it. Make a list of the opportunities presented by the change and communicate those opportunities to others in the organization.

Personality-related adaptability also entails remaining highly involved during times of change—not "checking out" emotionally or physically, staying excited and energetic, consistently and usefully contributing to brainstorming on new strategies, and successfully integrating into a new team or working across new organizational boundaries.

Leaders who are adept at the dispositional aspects of adaptability also encourage others in the organization or team to go with the flow of change. They elicit contributions from others, sincerely commend others for their innovative contributions, and make formal introductions of those who are new to the organization or team as a way of acknowledging that change has occurred and new group dynamics will emerge.

Emotional

It's all right for managers to admit resistance to change—in fact it's preferable, because emotions that are denied will eventually resurface and have to be dealt with. Resistance to change is natural; recognition and awareness of change are the keys to the emotional element of adaptability. Conceding your resistance to a change enables others in the organization to help you cope with the change. At the same time, it's important to not let emotions get the best of you, to maintain a balance, and to remain on task.

Addressing the emotions of others is a large part of the emotional component of adaptability. Managers should encourage others to express their emotions about a change—whether those feelings are positive or negative—and should not be critical of the expression of such emotions. One way to do this is to take thirty minutes each day for an organizational or group discussion and (with the aid of a flip chart) let everyone express his or her thoughts and feelings about the change that is occurring and the effect it is having.

OPPORTUNITY KNOCKS

Adaptability is not changing for changing's sake—it is responding to environmental factors in a way that has functional, effective results. Nor is adaptability easy. Staying positive and overcoming the fear and resistance that naturally accompany change can be difficult. (See "When People Are Set in Their Ways," on page 20.) In addition, a manager's cognitive adaptability won't be recognizable or influential if it is not expressly stated, so it's important for managers to communicate any new ideas or strategies they have to deal with a change. And even highly adaptive managers will be stifled if they are surrounded by colleagues who are stalwartly

When People Are Set in Their Ways

People's natural discomfort with and resistance to change—even change that may seem insignificant to others—was succinctly described by syndicated columnist Ellen Goodman in her 1979 book, *Turning Points*:

> "We cling to even the minor routines with an odd tenacity. We're upset when the waitress who usually brings us coffee in the breakfast shop near the office suddenly quits, and are disoriented if the drugstore or the cleaner's in the neighborhood closes. . . . We each have a litany of holiday rituals and everyday habits that we hold on to, and we often greet radical innovations with the enthusiasm of a baby meeting a new sitter."

Everyone can think of examples of the extent to which some people carry their aversion to change—some of these examples border on the absurd—and the sometimes crippling repercussions of refusing to or being unable to change. There are a number of tales, for example, about proprietors of traditional barbershops who steadfastly declined to adjust their enterprises during the 1960s trend toward unisex styling salons. As a result they watched their businesses go under. (There is a lot to be said for appreciating heritage, but clinging to tradition isn't worth much if it threatens survival.)

Alternative-medicine guru and author Caroline Myss has said that some people would rather die than change. In one extreme example of stubbornness toward change, a woman who was a confirmed lover of M&M's candies was shocked and infuriated when manufacturer Mars Inc. conducted a nationwide survey to determine whether to add a new color to M&M's. Believing that what wasn't broke shouldn't be fixed and that her favorite candy would never be the same, the woman sent letters of protest to Mars. But "blue" won out in the vote over "no change" (as well as "pink" and "purple"), and the woman has since refused to open another bag of M&M's. Because of her obsession with having things stay the same, she has forgone what used to be her favorite comfort food.

resistant to change and who discourage the expression of ideas and emotions related to change.

But the more positive experiences you have with change, the more you will become comfortable with and skilled at adaptability. So it's important not to shy away from change but instead take it on and look for the opportunities within it. For change, scary as it may seem, offers a chance to develop and progress not only on the organizational but also on the individual level.

Helping People Manage Transition

Kerry A. Bunker

The ongoing state of many contemporary organizations is one of change. Whether that change arises from economic, political, technological, cultural, or societal sources, its pace and complexity contribute to intense emotions that play out both inside and outside organizations. Such reactions as fear, insecurity, uncertainty, frustration, resentment, anger, sadness, depression, guilt, distrust, and a sense of unfairness and betrayal can make it difficult for leaders to set direction, encourage alignment, and gain commitment from the people in their organizations.

Moreover, leaders aren't immune to such reactions. Faced with the turmoil of change, many leaders fall back on managing organizational processes. They can fail to grasp the emotional aspects of change: grieving, letting go, building hope, and learning.

The reality is that different people can act differently and have different feelings about the changes they are experiencing. As a leader you should not expect your direct reports, peers, boss, or stakeholders to share your feelings but rather to act from their own points of view. At any given point in time, some will feel upbeat and energized, some anxious and tentative, and still others overwhelmed and numb. Some people may lack the requisite skills or experience needed to change and therefore will remain entrenched in old behavior; others may charge ahead with reckless abandon, seemingly oblivious to the changing demands. Still others will be upset and resistant in the short term but primed to recover and to learn over the long haul. The change leader's challenge is to recognize and understand the patterns of response that people express as they learn their way through transition and to customize intervention strategies that maximize the opportunity for individuals to bounce back from adversity and move forward in the evolving environment.

COMFORT AND CAPACITY

Simple principles often lie behind some of the most effective and promising ideas. This holds true in leading during times of change, even if simple principles don't or can't capture the full complexity and difficulty people experience when their organizations undergo transformation. To learn to lead more effectively in these circumstances, it's helpful to keep two principles in mind:

- If you want to lead people to somewhere new, you need to meet them where they are.
- Expect that some (even many) people aren't as far along as you would hope.

Assessing where people are in times of change involves observing the interaction between two important dimensions of their patterns of response: *comfort with change* (an openness and readiness to undertake new learning) and *capacity for change* (the ability to learn that which is required).

Powerful change injects an emotional dynamic into the equation. Encountering a meaningful change event signals that something that previously had value and seemed to be working is suddenly being called into question or stopped. Accepting and finding comfort with the change involves living through the emotional transition and coming to terms with aspects of the situation that are going away. An ending is required because people have to let go of the old ways and, by extension, elements of their old selves. As much as people's heads might desire to slip quickly and painlessly into the new circumstances, their hearts typically have a different agenda. It is often hard for people to be open and ready to take on the new challenges because in the past they have been successful at learning. Something they have mastered in earlier experiences has reinforced strategies and patterns of behavior that are now an established part of their repertoires and, as such, difficult to second-guess. As people feel the pressure to let go, the natural reaction is to deny what is happening and hope it will go away. When avoidance and denial fail to bring relief, instinct tells people to fight back and resist. Working their way through these rough periods of grieving and letting go opens the door to exploring the new opportunities and ultimately adapting to the change. Finding comfort with any given change can require different amounts of time for different people. Recognizing that individuals are working their way through this transition curve can enhance leaders' ability to offer the mix of challenge, support, and guidance that is most likely to trigger increases in readiness and openness to learning.

The good news and bad news is that life doesn't allow people to stand still. Each new change in their work and nonwork lives presents a test of people's underlying assumptions and an opportunity to examine and rethink their mental models for successful behavior. Old approaches and habits become ill-suited for addressing the evolving complexity that accompanies the changes in their lives. Yet the prospect of going against the grain of their preferred responses can trigger fears of loss and failure, which may in turn lead people to deny the existence of the new circumstance or at least to cling more tightly to entrenched behaviors and approaches that are no longer appropriate. Success in life is enhanced by the ability to learn, which in turn strengthens the capacity for change.

Unfortunately, knowing that the ability to learn is an important core competency doesn't make it easy to put that ability into practice. Indeed, going against the grain of established behavior generally results in a short-term drop in performance. Initial attempts to try out new behaviors are almost always less successful than responding in the old way. People can be reluctant to take on a new change simply because they sense there is a likelihood of looking bad or feeling vulnerable in front of others. There are stages in each new wave of the learning cycle where it feels easier and safer to deny or reject the emerging demands of change than to accept the risks inherent in testing out new and unfamiliar strategies and tactics.

FOUR PATTERNS

People who experience major organizational change tend to exhibit one of four patterns of response: *entrenched, overwhelmed, poser,* or *learner*. People can then pass through their initial stage and move to a stage that is more effective—especially if the leader provides timely intervention and support. Unfortunately, people can also revert to a less effective pattern if the leader fails to understand their situation or reacts too harshly to their transitional behavior. Leaders may not be happy with the stage, or group, that a direct report, a peer, or even their boss stands in, but that's where leaders must start too if they want to guide people toward a more effective response to the challenging situation. Although there is some overlap in the responses (what people feel, what actions they take, and how they learn) that are typical of each group, the constellation of responses among people in each group is quite distinct. It's important for leaders to remind themselves that individuals move in and out of these groups, a movement depending on such factors as the timing of events and each person's experiences, training, and comfort with specific issues.

Leaders' awareness of the four patterns of response to major organizational change can help them lead people during uncertain situations, but leading effectively depends on more than awareness—it depends on action. And although the leadership task of helping people not just survive but thrive in times of change may seem daunting, the odds will improve if leaders enter the situation knowing that each group has a different emotional response to confronting an uncertain future.

Entrenched Response

People operating in the entrenched mode tend to focus on riding out the change. They sense that the known and familiar

---

might be going away, which causes them to feel anxious and angry. They blame the organization for messing up what was working and try to keep their heads down until the leaders come to their senses. Consequently, they avoid taking risks. Typically, they can maintain their energy and continue to work hard, but they are narrow learners in the sense that they rely primarily on previously successful learning strategies and practices.

People in the entrenched group don't feel ready or able to make the transition, but they often have a suppressed capacity to do it, an ability that is much better than they realize. If the leader can support them in working through their emotions and guide them in accepting their capacity for change, the strength of this previously entrenched group can become a key leverage point for helping the organization ride out the transition.

To help the entrenched make a successful transition, leaders can

- Make sure these individuals can see what is actually going to change, by describing what will be different going forward.

- Help them see what they must let go of so they can face the ending they need to make to leave the old situation behind.

- Recognize that they will need continuous assistance through the ending and well into the new beginning.

- Express understanding and provide them with personal help to deal with stress, fear, and frustration.

- Provide carefully paced learning activities to teach new behaviors.

Overwhelmed Response

People in the overwhelmed group often report feeling depressed and powerless. The leader may see them withdrawing from what is going on around them. Because they are spending most of their energy trying not to think too much about what is happening, the overwhelmed have difficulty learning what is needed to survive in the new environment. Their negative mind-set can become infectious and inhibit the learning of others.

People in the overwhelmed group don't feel ready or able to make the transition. Their ability to make the transition may be limited, and their fear and withdrawal stand in the way of trying. But the leader needs to be cautious about judging too harshly or reacting too quickly. People with this response pattern often recover and learn their way to a healthier place. Getting them training and support can provide them with a foundation for participating more fully in the change.

To help the overwhelmed make a successful transition, leaders can

- Make sure these individuals can see what is actually going to change, by describing what will be different going forward.

- Help them see what they must let go of so they can face the ending they need to make to leave the old situation behind.

- Recognize that they will need continuous assistance through the ending and well into the new beginning.

- Express understanding and provide them with personal help to deal with stress, fear, and frustration.

- Provide a phased-in transition, with bridges to the old ways of doing things to the degree that is possible.

Poser Response

The poser pattern of behavior is often more enduring than the others and is linked to core elements of personality and experience. Posers often exhibit the same behaviors over long periods of time and across a wide range of situations. They express a high level of confidence about handling any change they encounter and are always eager to move on. But their competence and self-awareness fail to keep pace with their bravado and self-promotion. They jockey for positions of influence and recognition but do not learn well and may lead the organization in the wrong direction.

Posers, with their high levels of self-confidence and aggressive energy, probably feel more ready and able to make the transition than they really are. But their surface image and their underlying gap in learning capacity make them a significant threat to the organization. They tend to fool their leaders unless careful attention is focused on their actual performance and how they are perceived by others. The leader's best hope is to confront the posers' shortcomings with data and hold them accountable.

To help posers make a successful transition, leaders can

- Recognize that these individuals will be comfortable leaving the old behind and will seem confident in the new beginning zone, but that they need to be reined in.

- Provide external checks and balances to keep them on track, as they may lack self-awareness.

- Resist the urge to expand their role, even though they seem ready, willing, and able.

- Move cautiously toward new assignments, especially high-risk ones, and insist they embrace developmental learning.

Learner Response

People in the learner group feel challenged and stretched but in control of their own destinies. They look for opportunities in ambiguous and difficult situations and bounce back in the face of adversity. They seek learning opportunities to fill the gaps in their own development. In most organizations these individuals tend to be at the center of the action as change unfolds. Leaders may place excessive demands on them and look to them to be all things to all people.

Learners are ready and able to make the transition successfully—they can be the leader's allies. If the leader can help learners pass their outlook and their ability to learn along to people in other groups, the organization can adapt to change more successfully.

To help learners make a successful transition, leaders can

- Encourage and support these individuals' efforts.
- Give them high-impact roles with the latitude and resources to be successful.
- Make sure they have full knowledge of the big picture to provide needed context for their discussions and actions.

MOVING FORWARD

Today's organizations rank managing change and developing talent as two of the major keys to competitive advantage. To be successful, leaders need to understand people's patterns of response to change and customize intervention strategies to help the entire organization move forward.

Leading Yourself Through Change

Robert A. Goldberg

Does leading your organization through change have to feel like trudging through a swamp of molasses? We all say we want more collaboration, faster decisions, and more focus on customers than on internal politics. Yet it can be exasperating to see managers and employees desperately clinging to the way they have always done things, even as they nod in agreement about how things need to change.

What most leaders fail to recognize is that trying to change their organizations without first changing themselves simply doesn't work. To enable change beyond superficial window dressing, leaders must look at what they themselves are doing that keeps the organization stuck in the status quo. The enemy of change is often the fact that leaders do not look in the mirror. What they need is the courage to look.

TRAP SHOOTING

Leaders fall into three common traps as they attempt to guide their organizations through change. The first is expecting others to change without changing themselves.

Rick, the CEO of a consumer products company, complained that his highly paid vice presidents bounced decisions to him that they should have been making on their own. This prevented Rick from fulfilling the strategic aspect of his role, which included identifying potential acquisitions that would fuel growth.

Instead, Rick spent much of his time resolving internal squabbles. Ironically, his direct reports voiced similar complaints—their own staffs bickered constantly among themselves and rarely made decisions without the blessing of their vice president. This slowed the pace of new product introductions and stymied innovation.

What Rick didn't realize was that his own behavior had set the stage for these problems. For instance, in meetings he spent most of his time opposing others' points of view or criticizing team members for their bad decisions. He would often display impatience in dealing with a particular initiative, declare a quick solution, and delegate execution of the task.

When Rick wanted something done quickly he often delegated the task to two of his direct reports, who then tripped over each other in attempting to accomplish the objective. This was like throwing kerosene on a fire: departments withheld information from each other to curry favor and get Rick's attention.

But Rick's style of leadership caught up with him. The board of directors started applying more pressure on him to come up with a new acquisition target. The chairman confronted Rick over how he was spending his time—an incident Rick saw as an affront. It was not easy for such an aggressive and previously successful executive to receive such feedback.

It was only when Rick realized, deep down, that he couldn't continue down the path he was on and expect the company to be successful that he made some changes—not to others but to himself. First, he stopped attending planning meetings. Instead, he asked his executive team to recommend solid options to which he could respond. This forced the group to pull together as a team and not use Rick as an excuse for its lack of decisiveness.

Rick also stopped pitting his direct reports against each other. Rather, he clarified his and their roles and authority levels. Then he stuck to his commitments.

By changing his own behavior, Rick conditioned his direct reports to behave differently. As a result they collaborated with each other more, which led to less second-guessing of decisions. This resulted in faster and more innovative new product introductions, prompting Rick, ironically, to reconsider whether an acquisition was even necessary. After all, if internally generated new products could fuel growth and capture market share, why go outside?

Without a change in Rick's leadership style first, none of this would have happened. And Rick would have had only himself to blame for the organization's maintaining its unhealthy status quo.

MIND YOUR LANGUAGE

The second trap that many executives fall into in leading their organizations through change is being sloppy in describing what they want rather than precisely conveying what is needed and why.

Rhonda, for instance, was hired by a successful industrial company to establish a new marketing strategy. After two months her marketing plan still had not been approved, and Rhonda grew frustrated with what she considered the slow pace of change. She often remarked to others, "We need a revolution in marketing," or, "This marketing system is broken and it has to be fixed."

When Rhonda framed the change she sought in such dramatic language, her colleagues felt unfairly criticized. After all, they thought, who had given this newcomer, who hadn't earned her stripes, the right to judge them so harshly after they had been successful for so long? By failing to shape her language in terms that supported her agenda, Rhonda slowed rather than accelerated implementation of the marketing plan.

On a particularly difficult day, Rhonda shared her frustration with a colleague. Rather than accept Rhonda's complaints at face value, the colleague told Rhonda she was shooting herself in the foot with her attempts at influencing.

The colleague also questioned whether Rhonda's agenda was consistent with that of the company. When Rhonda reflected on her motives for taking the job in the first place, she realized that she had had a personal goal of making a big splash soon after joining the company. This ambition drove her to push harder than the situation required. After thinking it through, Rhonda began to change the language she used in attempting to influence others in the company. Although she still emphasized the need for change, she began to speak in less strident language. For instance, she referred to *evolution* and *tuning* rather than *revolution* and *fixing*. To her surprise, the pace of change accelerated once Rhonda cut some slack not only to herself but to others.

How executives talk about their work reflects their core intentions as well as how savvy they are about leading change. Language has a direct effect on others' behaviors and attitudes. By being mindful of the language they use, leaders can become more effective at implementing change. Without this level of thoughtfulness, executives risk undermining the very goals they desire.

SHIFTING APPROACH

The third trap that executives fall into in leading their organizations through change is mistaking natural resistance for total opposition.

Change is often threatening, particularly when it's imposed. Even something as seemingly innocuous as a new e-mail system causes people to lose the level of competence they had using the previous system. They must go through an uncomfortable transition as they learn something new. This leads to self-doubt and fear of looking bad—natural reactions when people are confronted with something unfamiliar. Unfortunately, leaders often mistake this natural resistance as total opposition.

When leaders mistake resistance as opposition, they tend to become heavy-handed in their efforts to make people implement and embrace change. People who feel steamrollered perceive a lack of respect from the leader, which can transform natural resistance into opposition. Thus, leaders create the very opposition they were hoping to avoid.

For example, Amy, the customer service manager for a health care products distribution company that was losing customers, was given the task of implementing handheld computer technology for managing inventory, to reduce process time and errors. But Amy's employees continued to use paper-and-pencil methods for inventory, claiming that the computer-based system was flawed and even slower than their earlier procedures.

At first Amy tried to sell her people on the benefits of the new technology. But when she became increasingly frustrated by their intransigence, she pushed them even harder. This led to the resignations of several good employees, and even lower productivity.

Finally, Amy realized that her people weren't totally opposed to the new system but were merely trying to hold on to what the old system had provided—the feelings of self-worth and mastery that come with performing a job well.

Amy changed her approach. She focused on ways to help her people preserve their feelings of confidence and self-esteem while they shifted to the new system. She had them continue to use the paper-and-pencil methods along with the computer system for a while, so they could feel good about their work while they learned the new process. She also stopped relying on the computer vendor to train her people in the new technology and had only her own employees who had learned the system act as trainers, reasoning that internal people would be less threatening. However, Amy also made it clear that phasing in the computer system was not negotiable.

These shifts in Amy's approach did the trick, and the new technology was soon embraced. But only by changing her own concept of resistance was Amy able to lead change effectively. Rather than seeing resistance as absolute opposition, she began to see it as a natural phenomenon—people holding on to something they valued while trying something new. This shift in Amy's mindset helped her see new options as a leader, and she could then apply the same approaches to other changes she wanted to make.

The task of changing organizations should not be taken lightly. People are too savvy to be manipulated with change-of-the-month initiatives or pep rallies exhorting them to change. In the final analysis, leaders need to consider how they themselves must change to get the results they seek. If they don't, there's no reason for them to expect their followers to embrace change any differently than they do now.

Change Factor: Making the Case for Executive Adaptability

Stu Kantor, Kathy E. Kram, and Fabio Sala

If the ability to lead and manage change is the great differentiator in today's increasingly fast-paced business environment, then executives who can adapt to change, rather than simply cope with it, will be the ones who consistently deliver outstanding results. A model to frame adaptability focuses on two dimensions: courage and curiosity. With motivation and opportunities, both can be developed.

Adaptability is no longer merely a leadership asset; it is a prime requirement. Adaptable leaders recognize that leading and managing change is the sine qua non of today's business world, and they urgently seek new ways to solve novel problems, master new skills, and embrace new challenges with grounded innovation. Such leaders are simultaneously optimistic and pragmatic. Employees who work with adaptable leaders can look to effective role models who embrace change as an opportunity to differentiate their organizations as cutting edge and responsive to their markets and clients. Without the ability to adapt rapidly to changing marketplace conditions, today's leaders are likely to be derailed—held in place, demoted, or even fired.

In this article we present a model that defines and frames adaptability, and we offer case examples to illustrate the model and the essential role that executive adaptability plays in today's constantly evolving business world. We outline a multidimensional approach to personal learning that articulates how and why adaptability can and must be developed by leaders who are truly committed to achieving consistent excellence.

TWO DIMENSIONS

A simple model to frame adaptability is based on two dimensions: *courage* and *curiosity*. True innovation and business process improvements require both these elements.

Courageous executives demonstrate alignment among their personal values, goals, and actions. They walk their talk, even when their point of view is unpopular. They demonstrate a willingness to challenge people, processes, and systems in the face of discontinuities among company values, goals, and actions.

Leaders who excel at interpersonal courage often form authentic relationships with their colleagues—the kind of relationships that generate deep emotional commitment to both individuals and the company. But these leaders also demonstrate the ability to make tough decisions regarding people while considering the best interests of the organization. Courage includes the capacity to

tolerate risk, ambiguity, and anxiety. Leaders high in courage welcome constructive criticism, admit and learn from their mistakes, and are aware of their own limitations.

Curiosity is an inherent desire to learn from every opportunity in one's environment. Curiosity drives leaders to ask questions that help them understand how new information affects their business, their customers, and their employees. It comes from an internal hunger to find out how and why things work the way they do, a passion for new experiences, and a desire for continuous learning. Curious executives search for root causes in pursuit of objectivity and optimal solutions. They are flexible, comfortable with change, and eager to harness diverse points of view. They seek feedback on their actions and use that feedback to guide their commitment to personal development.

These key dimensions of executive adaptability are seen in different degrees in four types of leaders: the Good Citizen (low courage and low curiosity), the Steadfast Visionary (low curiosity and high courage), the Creative Accommodator (low courage and high curiosity), and the Pioneer (high courage and high curiosity). The following case examples illustrate how courage and curiosity play out in the real world.

Case Example 1: The Good Citizen

Josh became a project manager at a groundbreaking Internet marketing company within eighteen months of his arrival. Because of his careful attention to detail, excellent people skills, and strong orientation toward results, he quickly advanced to positions of increasing responsibility and projects of greater visibility and strategic importance to the company. He developed a reputation for being able to motivate his teams to work long hours at a fast pace and consistently achieve ambitious goals. Not surprisingly, he was fast-tracked up the management ranks and was widely seen as having a great future.

However, Internet marketing is a constantly changing landscape, and Josh seemed unwilling or unable to experiment with new business models. Clients demanded innovation, and Josh appeared stuck on doing things in the same way that had brought him early career success. Senior executives became concerned that Josh was not looking forward or thinking strategically.

Josh came to be seen as a Good Citizen and a strong executor, one who led project teams competently and delivered solid work on time. But he did not demonstrate the ability or even an eagerness to anticipate marketplace changes and adapt accordingly—he seemed content to rely on his winning formula and to establish himself as an outstanding project manager who could be counted on to deliver operational excellence. Clearly missing from his repertoire of leadership capabilities were both the courage to tolerate the risk of potential mistakes and the curiosity to explore new ways of increasing market share.

Although Josh was a solid and reliable manager, the results of his shortcomings reveal the value of executive adaptability, of having a talent for transforming one's leadership style, actions, and strategy to meet changing business parameters. Great executives typically do one of two things well to create value for their companies: they either create truly new ways of doing things or they improve on existing strategies and processes. Both innovative and high-performance business cultures create environments that encourage curiosity and reward courage, and successful leaders model and exemplify these orientations. The key to driving continuous performance improvement is adapting one's current business strategy and execution process to changes in the marketplace.

Case Example 2: The Steadfast Visionary

Robert, a senior executive with a large airline company, had an impressive academic and employment pedigree. Although he was very bright, results oriented, and highly ambitious, he significantly underdelivered and eventually derailed.

He possessed the confidence that is critical for visionary leaders, but he was not open to feedback and input from important advisers, was stubborn, and did not alter his strategic vision in response to dramatic changes in the competitive environment of the airline industry. Ultimately he was unwilling and unable to learn how his basic assumptions about the business and himself were becoming obstacles to the future success of the business.

He was courageous and presented several forward-thinking ideas that moved the company ahead at critical points. However, he lacked curiosity about the root causes of change in the marketplace; he was committed to staying the course. Consequently, he missed critical cues and opportunities when the business could have adjusted to emerging market forces and competitive realities.

Case Example 3: The Creative Accommodator

Tom, the CEO of a high-tech organization he founded and ran for ten years, was well regarded by everyone in the company. The firm came into its own after the dot-com bubble burst, emerging as one of the most successful organizations in its class. Tom surrounded himself with executives in his image—people who were open-minded, genuine, and driven by a desire to break new ground in the industry.

Although Tom was successful in building the company, he had difficulty holding people accountable and could not adapt to shifting needs as the company matured into a highly focused, operationally efficient, results-oriented organization. Tom was high in curiosity—that was what helped him build such a successful company. However, his limited courage prevented him from adapting to do what was needed to take the company forward. He could understand and state what was required but could not act on it—he lacked the decisiveness that truly courageous leaders demonstrate. This ultimately led to a culture of mediocrity and underperformance.

INWARD AND OUTWARD

Adaptability is expressed both inwardly and outwardly. Internally expressed adaptability is driven by personal curiosity and courage. Executives have to reflect on their feelings and reactions to situations, fears, and desires in order to effectively manage their own motivations and their interactions with others.

Self-awareness is critical to both individual leadership effectiveness and organizational performance. A considerable degree of courage is necessary to explore honest feedback from others and openly examine one's own values, motivations, and behavior. Externally expressed adaptability is driven by an outward-focused curiosity and courage; such adaptability is observed in executives who scan and read external signals from colleagues, competitors, business operations, and the marketplace in order to respond effectively to the constantly changing business environment.

Naturally, executives vary in their capacities for both curiosity and courage. The Good Citizen is low on each of these dimensions, although he or she may be a competent manager of others and a company contributor, particularly in stable organizations. The Steadfast Visionary has courage but, because of a strong conviction to go with what he or she believes is right, may not think sufficiently outside the box to come up with new approaches. The Creative Accommodator is curious and can develop innovative strategies, but these strategies may not be recognized or seriously considered by the organization because of the leader's lack of courage. That brings us to the fourth type of leader.

Case Example 4: The Pioneer

As chief technology officer for a major health care services company, Sarah was highly curious—she was intense in her need for continuous learning. She not only frequently benchmarked best practices with industry peers but also read widely outside her own immediate discipline, applying lessons learned pragmatically and insightfully. For example, she drew on her college studies in Greek philosophy to further her desire to "know herself." She described herself as a lifelong learner. She was continuously looking for ways to understand and thereby uncover opportunities for change in strategic direction and performance improvements. Despite five quarters of double-digit growth for her company's flagship product, she introduced a major shift in the company's marketing strategy that she hoped would ensure growth well into the future.

Despite having achieved significant growth and improved organizational performance, Sarah continued to encourage and seek innovative approaches to strategic challenges to better serve clients. Her curiosity and courage drove her to continuous excellence.

Pioneers personify adaptability. They have sufficient courage to challenge existing business practices and the creative urge and the curiosity to think outside the box to come up with dramatically new ways of approaching current problems.

A mature organization operating in a relatively stable market will continue to perform well with a majority of its executives functioning as Good Citizens, but an entrepreneurial venture in a highly volatile and growing market will need an abundance of Pioneers to secure a first-mover advantage. Consequently, a critical step in a talent management process should be to assess whether the leadership core of the organization is made up of individuals with the right combination of curiosity and courage to successfully meet current and ever-changing business needs and challenges.

OPPORTUNITY KNOCKS

A senior executive team in one organization recognized the curiosity and courage of a young executive and decided to promote him very quickly, with the expectation that he would be able to handle the challenge. As a result of the executive team's confidence in this leader and his ability, he was given the opportunity to take on a strategically important role. He delivered excellent results and strengthened the leadership core of the organization. Here is how it happened.

The Adaptable Leader

When Jackson was promoted to the chief operating officer position in a global financial services firm from two levels down in the sales organization, he leapfrogged over a dozen natural candidates for the job. His colleagues and competitors for the COO role saw him as a knowledgeable and engaging salesperson and viewed his success as largely a function of his tireless energy and boundless optimism.

Most people doubted his ability to succeed in his new role; they thought he was far too green to manage multiple products and services across a wide range of businesses. They didn't realize how excited and motivated he was by his challenge or how committed he was to reaching his full potential.

Jackson knew everyone saw him as a prototypical salesperson and understood that perception as reasonable. After all, he had spent his entire seventeen-year career in sales and sales management. What people did not realize was that Jackson's career was grounded in sales because he saw an opportunity to progress quickly in that field, not because he lacked ability or interest in other aspects of business. What others also didn't appreciate was that Jackson was strikingly realistic about his strengths and weaknesses and fascinated by every aspect of his company. He was well aware of the risk he was taking by leaving the security of the deep relationships he had built with customers and his sales support team, but he demonstrated the curiosity and courage needed to take on a broader set of responsibilities. Fortunately, several senior executives were fully aware of his passion and commitment to both the company and his professional development.

Soon after he was promoted, Jackson participated in an executive development program that included both functional learning and one-to-one leadership coaching. He brought the same energy and open-minded curiosity to his personal development and the COO role that he had brought to every new sales relationship. He leveraged those relationship skills to improve collaboration across all business units. He relied on his deep understanding of clients' needs to relentlessly drive clients' perspectives into every product and service the company offered. After three years as COO, he was appointed president and CEO of the firm.

FROM WITHIN

Few would argue that executive adaptability is not an important leadership competency, but some may believe that adaptability is a static personality trait rather than a learnable business skill. They may also believe that people can't do much about low levels of curiosity and courage. But even those seriously lacking in courage or curiosity, or both, can enhance their capacity to adapt—if they possess sufficient desire to do so.

We believe that enduring personal change originates *within* each individual. Many executives are skeptical about leadership development efforts; they are often reluctant to change what they see as the tried-and-true strategies that brought them where they are.

We also believe that leaders require accurate self-assessment, honest and constructive feedback, strong motivation, challenging opportunities, and the chance to practice their newly developing capabilities inside their real work settings (as opposed to the classroom) to achieve their highest potential. We have found that to develop adaptability in a rigorous and systematic way at the individual and organizational level, executives need a combination of individual study (such as executive coaching and mentoring assignments), action learning (such as peer coaching and project-based assignments), leadership development programs (such as competency-based training programs and case studies), real work assignments to broaden perspectives (such as job rotations, task force assignments, and job sharing), and alignment of organizational processes (such as performance management that rewards and encourages adaptability). All of these things create a *learning infrastructure* that provides executives with a rich source of experiences that cultivate their adaptability as leaders.

COACHING UP

An executive coaching relationship can provide the structured environment necessary for real development and personal change. An effective coaching relationship enables executives to explore themselves and their ways of doing business with a professional who understands both organizational life and behavioral science.

Establishing an effective coaching relationship is no small feat. The coach's professional credibility alone is not sufficient. Rigorous data collection, including numerous interviews and 360-degree-assessment surveys, provides a vehicle for launching a meaningful collaborative relationship. Businesspeople respect solid data and individuals who do their homework thoughtfully and thoroughly. A coach's knowledge of the client coupled with a commitment to the developmental process builds a bridge of common purpose and trust.

This approach to executive development must be strategically tailored to real-life performance goals and organizational success. Otherwise it is unlikely that the organization's culture and practices will support the individual's efforts to develop adaptability. The coaching client's organization must benefit in observable and measurable ways.

Many leadership development programs occur in classroom settings where 360-degree feedback is generated and individuals have the opportunity to examine these data with the help of a development professional. During these programs, participants are encouraged to reflect on their leadership capabilities and to plan for their continuing development beyond the classroom experience. With specific developmental goals and action plans in hand, participants move forward with clear opportunities to practice new behaviors and attitudes.

ONGOING LEARNING

Executive coaching and relational learning among peers—in the context of educational programs and as stand-alone initiatives—are powerful interventions when it comes to developing executive adaptability. However, years of experience and research have shown that onetime interventions are not sufficient to ensure that leaders will not relapse into old behaviors and routines in the face of challenges and crises at work.

Organizations that acknowledge the need to make their leaders more adaptable should consider how to encourage a culture that makes ongoing personal learning an important priority and relatively accessible to organizational members at all levels. Leaders armed with new self-awareness and insight into behaviors that will enhance their effectiveness in leadership roles must establish practices back at work that encourage regular reflection on experiences, alone and in dialogue with others. An essential ingredient of continuous learning and the development of executive adaptability is the formation of a *personal board of advisers*. This board, chosen by the executive, consists of a handful of individuals inside and outside the immediate work environment whom the executive trusts and regularly consults for feedback and counsel.

QUESTIONS TO ASK

Leaders can improve their adaptability—their capacities for both courage and curiosity—if the necessary conditions for personal learning are in place. Challenging assignments combined with opportunities to reflect with others who are willing and able to provide honest and constructive feedback, coaching, and support create a powerful developmental process.

A continuous learning culture enables both individuals and organizations to recognize how they can improve the essential executive capability of adaptability. Successful leadership and organizational development strategies include opportunities for assessment, practice of new behaviors in combination with ongoing support and encouragement, timely feedback, and rewards for development and execution of innovation and business performance improvement.

Are mechanisms in place to provide executives with regular and valid feedback on the effects of their behaviors at work? Does the organizational culture encourage and respect learning from mistakes? Are executives given opportunities for periodic retreats from the action to find space for reflection and renewal? These are some of the questions that must be asked by leaders who want to encourage executive adaptability.

When these questions are adequately addressed, organizations will be able to develop the leadership talent needed to effectively address key strategic challenges. Courage and curiosity will drive innovation and change, and both individual and organizational performance will rise to new heights.

Flexible Flyers:
A Leader's Framework
for Developing Adaptability

Allan Calarco and Joan Gurvis

In today's business world the complexity and pace of
change can be daunting. In this environment of rapid
change, leaders are coming to recognize that they need to
develop adaptability to be effective. The process of developing
adaptability begins with learning and practicing three types
of flexibility—cognitive, emotional, and dispositional.

Leaders all over the world are facing unprecedented challenges:
new cultures, new jobs, new markets, new everything. Dramatic
change often creates feelings of uncertainty, self-consciousness,
and even fear. Most leaders know from experience that even minor
change can have a powerful effect.

Given the current complexities of work, the sheer volume
of information flowing in, and the rapid changes taking place, it
makes sense for leaders—and the people they lead—to be adaptable. Adaptability is no longer a nicety or a coping mechanism—it
is a leadership imperative. Without the ability to adapt to change,
leaders previously seen as successful and filled with potential are
likely to be derailed—fired, demoted, or held on a career plateau.

Many of the challenges facing organizations today are adaptive challenges—systemic challenges with no clear-cut solutions.
Whereas technical challenges require redistributions of resources
and well-defined plans of action, systemic challenges involve creating new processes, systems, or skills. The increased complexity of
today's organizational challenges requires leaders to work in new
ways. They need to be skilled adapters.

THREE ELEMENTS

So it's a given that today's leaders need to respond effectively to change in the organizational environment. But what is it that allows some leaders to adjust better to change than others? The answer involves three components:

Cognitive flexibility: the ability to use a variety of thinking strategies and mental frameworks

Emotional flexibility: the ability to vary one's approach to dealing with one's own emotions and those of others

Dispositional flexibility (or personality-based flexibility): the ability to remain optimistic and at the same time realistic

This three-part framework of adaptability was developed in 1999 by Steve Zaccaro, a professor of psychology at George Mason University. Subsequent research conducted by Zaccaro, Paige Bader, and Cary Kemp in the context of CCL's Looking Glass Experience program confirmed this framework. These studies identified specific behaviors tied to each component and found that having just one of these characteristics is not sufficient for leader adaptability.

Leaders must exhibit two of the three characteristics to be perceived as adaptable. Scoring high on all three components indicates that a leader is highly adaptable.

Adaptability can be developed. All three types of flexibility can be learned and improved by practicing the behaviors tied to each. The more adept a person is at being cognitively, emotionally, and dispositionally flexible, the more adaptable he or she will be in leadership roles.

Cognitive Flexibility

Leaders who have cognitive flexibility are able to incorporate a variety of thinking strategies and mental frameworks into their planning, decision making, and managing of day-to-day work. Someone who works Plan A while having Plans B, C, and D in mind is cognitively flexible. He or she can simultaneously hold multiple scenarios in mind and can see when to shift and inject a change. Cognitive flexibility indicates nimble and divergent thinking, an interest in developing new approaches, the ability to see and leverage new connections, and the propensity to work well across the organization. Leaders with cognitive flexibility readily learn from experience and recognize when old approaches don't work.

Recognizing the characteristics of leaders with cognitive flexibility is one thing, but what is it that these leaders actually do? Research shows that they tend to do three key things:

Scan the environment. Leaders need to be able to identify changes as they occur. It is critical for them to know the context of their business environment so they will be able to discern new trends and opportunities and not be caught by surprise. Managers who are successful at scanning the environment continuously solicit information about relevant factors from knowledgeable sources and, more important, use that knowledge to reshape their understanding and perspectives. They are able to acknowledge that a change has occurred and can visualize how it will affect the organization.

Develop understanding by engaging in sense making. Detecting coming change is the first key to cognitive flexibility; understanding it is the second. Managers need to diagnose and interpret the meaning of changes for themselves and their units. Sense making, the process of developing a collective understanding of a situation, is important for adequately interpreting and comprehending information. Seemingly dissimilar views often result in powerful opportunities for change once each person or group has come to a full and shared view. This process may include divergent thinking—for instance, contemplating a totally new direction that turns an obstacle into an opportunity or an old idea into an innovative practice. Dialogue—conversation balanced by advocacy and inquiry—is a powerful tool for creating shared meaning among teams and individuals.

Create strategies. Managers need to respond strategically to environmental changes. When doing so they should develop several possible strategies, recognizing that it is impossible to predict exactly how a situation will play out. Cognitive adapters are able to move beyond strategies that have worked in the past because they understand that these strategies may not work in the present. In fact cognitive adapters seek out or test new approaches. They also devise varying strategies for leading. In particular they find different ways to communicate their interpretations of changing events and the needed responses. The ability to persuade effectively and address the emotional aspects of change becomes critical.

Emotional Flexibility

Leaders with emotional flexibility vary their approach to dealing with their emotions and those of others—an area that many leaders often fail to consider. An emotionally flexible leader is comfortable with the process of transition, including grieving, complaining, and resistance. Adapting to change requires give-and-take between the leader and those experiencing the change. A leader without emotional flexibility is dismissive of others' concerns or emotions and shuts down discussion. An emotionally adaptive leader, however, moves the change or agenda forward. He or she doesn't "give in" to emotions or get pulled off course by concerns.

Demonstrating emotional flexibility requires leaders to do the following:

Understand and manage their own emotions. Being emotionally flexible requires leaders to first demonstrate an awareness of their own emotions. This means acknowledging and presenting their emotional responses in an authentic way, thereby helping others to do the same. Leading is emotionally difficult work. Leaders who ignore the emotional element and deal only with the "reality" will be less effective and will eventually suffer from the strain. As a leader you will need energy and fortitude to deal with change; care of your emotional self can help you maintain the necessary vigor.

Connect with and address the emotions of others. Emotionally flexible leaders are aware of what subordinates and peers are feeling. They need to consider this emotional aspect and respond to it in helpful and positive ways. Being open and forthright, along with creating a safe space for people to express their emotions, goes a long way toward gaining commitment.

Engage emotionally to help others get on board. In the midst of change, leaders often assume that people will automatically be motivated and engaged. What they fail to realize is that others may be resisting or in denial. By acknowledging the reality of the situation with genuine emotion and support, leaders can encourage others to connect with the change and stay engaged. It is impossible to move through a transition when colleagues are apathetic and disconnected.

Maintain a balance between emotion and action. Empathy and good listening are key; emotionally flexible leaders find a balance between allowing enough time for the struggle and helping to resolve it and move on. They allow the expression of negative emotions and also discourage wallowing in them.

Dispositional Flexibility

Leaders who display dispositional flexibility operate from a place of optimism grounded in realism and openness. They acknowledge a bad situation but simultaneously visualize a better future. Such leaders figure out what they need to be optimistic about in the current context, no matter what the difficulties and challenges. They are neither blindly positive nor pessimistic and defeatist. Ambiguity is well tolerated. Dispositionally flexible leaders see change as an opportunity rather than as a threat or danger.

Dispositional flexibility can be seen when leaders engage in the following actions:

Show genuine and realistic optimism about change, and communicate that optimism to others. Leaders who are dispositionally flexible are confident that both they and the team can be effective in the new environment. They identify what is positive about the new experience or situation and build on it.

Balance expressions of uncertainty with a positive attitude. Effectively communicating with others and focusing on the positive must be balanced with realism and a willingness to give voice to uncertainty. Dispositionally flexible leaders allow others to understand the questions and issues behind their concerns and doubts. This can often lead to constructive brainstorming and conversations and frequently will uncover new approaches and solutions.

Support others through the process of change. Leaders who are adept at the dispositional aspects of flexibility encourage others in the organization or team to go with the flow of change. They elicit contributions from others, sincerely commend others for their innovative contributions, and introduce those who are new to the organization or team in order to acknowledge that change has occurred and new group dynamics will emerge. They are highly visible and energetic.

Know their own tendencies related to change. Dispositionally flexible leaders demonstrate an awareness of their own preferences and behaviors but are able to modify these tendencies as needed. They are comfortable experiencing new things, trying new approaches, and working through ambiguity.

A CHANCE TO GROW

In today's business environment change is fast and constant. For leaders the implications are both personal and organizational—and the consequences of not adapting to change can be severe. The key is to embrace change and use it as an opportunity to grow and learn. The more positive experiences that leaders have with change, the more they become comfortable with and skilled at adaptability. The process of developing adaptability begins with leaders learning about and deepening their cognitive, emotional, and dispositional flexibility.

Knowing Change Preferences Is a Boon for Leaders

Christopher Musselwhite

How people deal with change—both creating it and responding to it—is a function of identifiable individual preferences. Whether people see change as a danger, a challenge, or an opportunity, they have individual preferences that reflect their relationship to structure, rules, and authority.

Gaining knowledge of these preferences can enable leaders to manage groups and organizations more effectively in situations of change and to better understand disagreements with others in such situations. Leaders can leverage this knowledge to create the powerful advantage of collaboration—directing collective energy into creating and producing desired outcomes rather than letting it go into blaming, defending, and fighting about the change process itself.

For ages people have debated over the best way to approach change. People in various arenas, from politics to economics and from business to education, have argued over evolution versus revolution, incrementalism versus innovation, reform versus reinvention, and total quality management versus reengineering. Often these debates have had an either-or quality; one approach is right and the other is wrong. Such a framework for change frequently produces conflict, misunderstanding, strong-arming, and missed opportunities—not the outcomes envisioned by the change initiators.

Taking the time to understand the contributions of each of three individual change style types—*conservers, pragmatists,* and *originators*—can help leaders become better at recognizing and managing the effective and ineffective behaviors of each preference and, as a result, at facilitating collaboration and teamwork.

THE EVOLUTIONISTS

At one end of the change style continuum are the conservers. They are good at defining and clarifying current reality. Working together to build on what is already working is the preferred path to change for a conserver.

To create improvements, conservers prefer working within existing policies, processes, and procedures.

Conservers favor a total quality management and continuous improvement approach to organizational change. They may, in fact, see the need for substantial systemic changes but prefer to make such changes gradually. Conservers want to keep the current system working smoothly and will resist decisions and efforts that they perceive will create chaos.

Conservers will ask the hard questions of proposed change: How will this be better than what we have now? Why is the standard practice we have followed all this time no longer acceptable? Who will be affected by this proposed change? What are the political implications of the change? What will this cost? What is the return on investment? What is the loss in organizational productivity and effectiveness resulting from these changes?

Used effectively, these questions are beneficial to any organization undergoing change. Used ineffectively, they create the appearance of obstruction and foot-dragging.

THE SITUATIONALISTS

Pragmatists tend to focus more on viable results—getting the job done—than on challenging or preserving existing structures. They often see merit in both an evolutionary and a revolutionary approach and are motivated more to find adequate and timely solutions to problems than to advance ideologies.

Eric Schmidt, currently executive chairman of Google, was appointed CEO of networking software maker Novell in 1997.

He faced a daunting turnaround—the company was in dire straits, with Microsoft's Windows NT operating system competing aggressively for the same market. In the face of this crisis, Schmidt said his biggest challenge was retaining the smartest employees. His strategy was captured in a 2001 *Harvard Business Review* interview:

> *I've found that the best way to manage smart people is to let them self-organize so they can operate both inside and outside the management hierarchy. They report to a manager but they also have the latitude to work on projects that interest them, regardless of whether they originate with their own manager. You tell them: "Look, I don't know how to solve this problem, so why don't you throw yourself at it and figure it out? Take the time and resources you need, and get it right." If they get frustrated and need to blow off steam, you invite them to talk with you directly—no go-betweens. At the same time, you discuss this new component of the person's work directly with his or her manager, and there are no reprisals when a smart person works outside a manager's jurisdiction.*

Pragmatists tend to focus on the actions required to move a situation from the current or past reality toward a new desired outcome. They want to solve problems and bring plausible ideas into reality. They tend to seek a balanced inquiry through an exploration of multiple perspectives.

THE REVOLUTIONARIES

Originators like to challenge current structures and systems. They encourage the exploration of new and alternative ideas and suggest possibilities that others have not imagined. Strategy guru Gary Hamel is a strong advocate of revolutionary change. In his book *Leading the Revolution* (Harvard Business School Press, 2000), he writes:

> *We live in a world where precedent has lost much of its imperial power. Rather than wasting energy in defending incrementalism*

against an imagined foe, corporate leaders should be working to build an innovative pipeline that is chock full of the kind of precedent-busting ideas that have the power to transform industries and to create new wealth. Oh, and on a final word to shareholders: Beware of the CEOs whose ambitions stretch no further than the incremental.

Originators tend to focus on new possibilities, vision, and direction. They encourage organizations to begin new tasks sooner rather than later. They often show a propensity for action but may not be effective implementers.

FREQUENT ENCOUNTERS
The three change style preferences fall along a linear continuum extending from conservers at one extreme to originators at the other, with pragmatists in the middle. About 25 percent of the general population are conservers and another 25 percent are originators; the rest are pragmatists.

Change style preferences are collections of beliefs, attitudes, behaviors, and thought processes that describe how people accept, manage, and instigate change. People encounter these preferences in various degrees every day in their dealings with others and exhibit their own preferences just as readily when faced with an opportunity for change.

Now that we know the characteristics of conservers, pragmatists, and originators, let's explore how they deal with change.

Conservers prefer to work within the existing structure and to create incremental changes. When facing change, conservers

- Generally appear deliberate, disciplined, and organized.
- Prefer change that maintains the current structure.
- May operate from conventional assumptions.
- Enjoy predictability.

- May appear cautious and inflexible.
- Honor tradition and established practice.

Here's a scenario that we can use to compare the typical viewpoints of conservers, pragmatists, and originators.

You are headed home late at night on a familiar stretch of highway. Yours is the only car on the road. As you approach the intersection the light changes from green to yellow. You feel a momentary frustration because you know from experience that this light has a long cycle and seems to stay red forever. What do you do?

If you are a conserver, you regard traffic lights as essential. Conservers appreciate the rules and value traffic lights for what they represent (a system for ensuring safety and order). They value the rules not so much for the sake of rules but for what rules represent. They know that without rules to guide drivers, roads would be chaotic places. Traffic lights bring order to the roadways and ensure against chaos. As a consequence, conservers will likely sit through a red light late at night with no other cars in sight and wait patiently until the light changes before proceeding.

Conservers also

- Prefer gradual and incremental change. They are evolutionists rather than revolutionists. They want to see the existing structure retained with improvements. They prefer to solve problems and to improve efficiency while maintaining the continuity and stability of current systems and structure.

- Prefer a secure work environment that is free from unexpected disruptions and surprise changes. They prefer predictability and are attracted to stable, structured, and orderly workplaces. They like to be rewarded for contributing at a steady and consistent pace. They appreciate having the time and a place for reflection.

- Appear disciplined and organized. They notice details and act deliberately. They know the rules, regulations, and policies of the domains in which they live and work. They prefer to live by these rules.

- Prefer tested and proven solutions. They look for proven examples of what has worked elsewhere. They want to see a track record with evidence of effective performance. They embrace tradition and convention and rely on the predictability that experience affords.

Pragmatists deal in outcomes and seek practical, functional solutions to problems. When facing change, pragmatists

- May appear practical, agreeable, and flexible.
- Operate as mediators and catalysts for understanding.
- Are open to both sides of an argument.
- May take a middle-of-the-road approach.
- Appear team oriented.

Pragmatists respect the purpose of the traffic light but also appreciate when it is appropriate and when it is not. Late at night, with no other cars in sight, a pragmatist is likely to come to a full stop, look carefully for cross traffic and for a police car, then proceed. Pragmatists do not object to breaking the rules on moral grounds; they just want to ensure that the purpose of the rule has been served and that they do not get caught. For the pragmatist, the go-no-go decision may not be so much about the merits of traffic lights and laws as it is about the consequences of breaching the rules.

Pragmatists also

- Are the peacemakers and the middle-of-the-roaders. They seek compromise to arrive at a solution that provides a workable outcome. If necessary, they will settle for a solution that is less than optimal rather than be stuck in a no-action situation.

- Often appear to be reasonable and practical. They listen to supporting arguments and look for practical results that accomplish the intended goals, often without regard to politics or egos.

- Are usually agreeable and flexible. They can see arguments from different perspectives and can value the contributions of others. At the same time, their flexibility may allow them to be pulled in many directions and can appear to be indecisive. In their willingness to seek a compromise position, pragmatists sometimes appear to be noncommittal. Others may regard them as too quick to compromise.

- Like change that emphasizes practical and workable outcomes. They focus on the results and the effective functioning of the organizational system rather than on the organizational structure or politics. If adjusting the existing structure rather than reengineering it presents a workable solution, pragmatists will favor this solution because it is faster to implement. If the simple solution is not workable, they will readily accept making a more radical change.

- Appear to be more team oriented than do either conservers or originators. Pragmatists are interested in hearing all ideas and getting everyone's perceptions on the table for the group's consideration.

- Are less likely than originators or conservers to have hidden agendas. Pragmatists tend to have fewer axes to grind and points to prove than those who are committed to maintaining or challenging the status quo.

- Are mediators. Because pragmatists see the views of both conservers and originators, they often serve as bridges of understanding between the two groups. The merit they are willing to grant to both perspectives also supports their unique role in bridging between factions and in providing objective critiques.

- Like an action-oriented workplace that engages others in a harmonious and participative atmosphere. Pragmatists prefer an environment that is flexible and adaptive, one that responds to current pressures. They also like to be involved in hands-on experiences rather than theoretical discussions. They want adequate opportunities to discuss various options with coworkers. When harmony is not possible, pragmatists may withdraw from the debate or settle for a less-than-optimal solution.

Originators sometimes favor something that's different simply because it is different. When facing change, originators

- May appear unorganized, undisciplined, unconventional, and spontaneous.
- Prefer change that challenges current structure.
- Will likely challenge accepted assumptions.
- Enjoy risk and uncertainty.
- May appear visionary and systemic in their thinking.
- May be impractical and miss important details.
- Can treat accepted policies and procedures with little regard.

Originators see the traffic light as serving the specific purpose of controlling traffic so people do not get hurt. They respect the purpose, not the rule. From their perspective, the traffic light imposes limitations on their freedom to drive. These limitations are acceptable to them when danger is present. If they do not perceive that a danger is present, then the traffic light has no intrinsic value to them. They believe they should not be penalized for moving through the red light if no cars are coming. "I can decide when it's safe to proceed," they say.

Originators also

- Prefer quick and expansive change. They favor revolution over evolution. They approach life as an imperative to discard the old and to bring in the new as often and as quickly as possible. They will add to and build on the ideas of others, taking the thinking in directions that others may not see as helpful or connected, even though the originator's logic makes perfect sense to him or her.

- Are often viewed in organizations as change agents. They may be the ones who cause new things to happen and encourage goals to be accomplished in new ways.

- Tend to loathe repetitive tasks. Doing the same job in the same way with the expectation of getting the same result holds no charm for originators. When a job does not require creativity or ingenuity, they may look for an alternative way to do the job. If they cannot find one, they may abandon the job.

- May appear to be undisciplined and unconventional. They may seem to be making up rules as they go along and perhaps experimenting. Desks may be cluttered and work spaces chaotic, suggesting disorganization. However, an originator can often reach into an overwhelming pile of papers and books and produce the very document he or she was asked to retrieve. Originators may simply have a different system of organization.

- Often challenge existing assumptions, rules, and regulations. Tradition and history are of less value to originators than are future possibilities.

- Are often regarded as visionary, out-of-the-box thinkers. They frequently attempt to solve problems in ways that challenge existing norms. They tend to favor the new and the different, the innovative and the adventurous. They like to try untested solutions, convinced by their own evaluations that these ideas will work.

- May appear to be impulsive. They are often ready and eager to move ahead, even though it appears that they have not closely considered the consequences of the proposed change. Originators may take new and unexpected directions.

- Are risk takers. They are willing to take a calculated risk to test out new methods and approaches when they are convinced of an idea's value.

EACH ADDS VALUE

Although leaders may be closely described by the characteristics of a particular change style, they are not limited to only those behaviors, attitudes, values, and beliefs. Change styles are preferences. As is the case with left-handedness or right-handedness, leaders have distinct and natural preferences, but they also maintain the capacity to develop other skills through conscious effort.

To consciously choose to behave differently, leaders must first be aware of their personal preferences. With that awareness, they can practice behaviors that are appropriate for the situation at hand, as opposed to unconsciously doing whatever comes naturally. Effective leaders realize that no one change style is better than another or more preferable from an organization's perspective. Indeed, each change style preference adds value to the organization when it is used and managed effectively.

Leading a Changing Workforce: Lessons from the U.S. Army

Gene Klann

The end of the military draft and the transition to a force of all volunteers posed a huge reengineering challenge for the U.S. Army. The challenge was made even more acute by budget cuts and downsizing. The principles the Army followed to emerge as a strong, effective organization provide a road map for civilian organizations that are also grappling with dramatic change.

After the Vietnam War, with the move from a draft-based to an all-volunteer force (AVF), the U.S. Army faced a formidable challenge: maintaining and improving itself while dealing with a changing workforce. In meeting this challenge, the Army followed several important principles that can be of value for other organizations today as they, too, strive for excellence with a dynamic workforce.

The transition to an AVF caused a dramatic cultural shift in the Army. It became a highly diverse organization with a large percentage of women, African Americans, and Hispanic Americans. This force was notably successful in the first Gulf War, but with the end of the Cold War the Army had to go through a downsizing of 600,000 soldiers and a budget cut of more than 40 percent. At the same time it was performing peacekeeping, disaster relief, and nation-building missions in places such as Bosnia, Haiti, Kosovo, Rwanda, and Somalia; continuing a presence in South Korea, Panama, and Kuwait and with NATO in Western Europe; and maintaining a high state of readiness for combat—the Army's raison d'être. This was all done during a period of extended U.S. economic prosperity, which increased the difficulty of recruiting and retaining soldiers. The principles the Army followed, however, enabled it to not only survive but thrive.

CHOOSE GOOD PEOPLE

High-performing organizations must have high-quality personnel. The standards of the draft had been notoriously low. For the AVF, personnel selection standards were constantly reviewed and upgraded. One key was to accept primarily high school graduates as volunteers. This standard went a long way toward lowering attrition rates and improving discipline and training overall.

TREAT PEOPLE WELL

Because the battlefield is a harsh and brutal place, Army leadership traditionally believed that military indoctrination and initial training should also be harsh and brutal. This approach, which gave us the stereotypical images of the screaming drill sergeant, the relationally challenged colonel, and the badly harassed first-year West Point cadet, had been taken with the best interests of the soldiers in mind: to help them survive in combat. But during the Vietnam War this approach no longer seemed to work so well. The need to go through tough and demanding training to prepare for combat was generally understood, but soldiers openly wondered why they couldn't be treated with respect and dignity while being trained.

The Army realized that adjusting the approach to training so it acknowledged the dignity of people would lead to more committed and therefore better soldiers. The new, better-educated recruits, in particular, would expect better treatment and would respond to it.

FOCUS ON CORE VALUES

The Army determined that it had lost its focus on its primary mission: *combat*. To remedy this problem, Army leadership placed renewed emphasis on the vision of combat readiness in peace and victory in war.

The leadership also established a set of core values as the foundation for a force in which large-scale and rapid transferal of personnel was the norm. (In my twenty-five-year Army career, for example, I made thirteen major moves.) These values include purpose, people, responsibility, and integrity. They are intended to give personnel a sense of continuity and stability amid a culture of changing tasks and global assignments.

Two additional principles support this principle of focusing on core values:

1. A clear and realistic vision is necessary to keep the entire organization focused and moving in the same direction.

2. A clear and constantly emphasized set of core values is essential to ensuring organizational continuity, stability, and efficiency.

DEFINE KEY ACTIVITIES

Another way that the Army kept itself on track was by establishing six imperatives: leadership development, a quality force, the right mix of personnel, modern equipment, doctrine, and training. Whereas values are focused on maintaining a connection with what is good about the past, imperatives provide a focus for the present and, more important, a practical view of the future. Imperatives were a great help in making the vision a reality.

Here is a look at how the Army acted on two of these imperatives.

Leadership Development

The Army has a lot of leaders. There are hundreds of them in a 15,000-soldier division, so leadership development must be a high priority. Leadership development in the Army has three pillars: education and training, on-the-job experience, and self-development.

Leadership development for both officers and noncommissioned officers was expanded. New courses were established and old ones upgraded. At the higher levels, assessment-for-development instruments such as the Myers-Briggs Type Indicator were introduced. The Army also created innovative assessment surveys that focus on getting a fix on the command climate in battalion-size units.

An assessment-for-development process is now conducted after major training activities. In the *after-action review* (AAR), all the key players involved in the training meet. With a set of clear guidelines and a facilitator, they discuss what went well, what could be improved, what lessons were learned, and whether previously successful methods were validated. At first the AAR was referred

---

to cynically as "the autopsy," but after Army leadership took steps to ensure that the focus was on fixing problems and not on placing blame, the AAR feedback process became a key element in the effective operation of the Army.

Training

Army training, which is vital to combat readiness, has been totally revamped. Both units and individual soldiers are now expected to be ready for combat. Therefore, in the move to the AVF, physical training was accelerated, weight standards were tightened, and personnel were routinely tested for drug use. Unit training standards were raised. Field training was made more realistic, challenging, and adventurous. Training areas such as the National Training Center were created. The center is an area of California desert the size of Rhode Island where Army units hold war games. Soldiers and combat vehicles use nonlethal laser weapons, making the training extremely realistic.

It is understood in the Army that training needs to be continuous, not a one-time event. Essential information is presented with three R's in mind: review, repeat, and reinforce. Also, training is aimed at soft (relational) skills as well as hard (technical) skills. Soft skills include the basic people and social skills that the military had ignored for years, perhaps centuries. In the final analysis, soft skills are potentially the most difficult to master but have the highest impact.

JUST ONE THING

In the movie *City Slickers*, a grizzled old cowboy named Curly proclaims that "just one thing" is important in life. He refuses, however, to say exactly what that thing is. We have seen that a combination of factors is responsible for the success of the Army's AVF, but if that success were to be attributed to just one thing, what would it be?

There is a strong hint in the book *Hope Is Not a Method: What Business Leaders Can Learn from America's Army* (Times Business, 1996), cowritten by General Gordon Sullivan, who was chief of staff of the Army from 1991 to 1995, and his chief planner, Colonel Michael Harper. The book outlines the Army's processes, methods, and management techniques that brought about much of the post-Vietnam transformation. One theme is the Army's unwavering emphasis on the human dimension in all its transition processes. Consider this excerpt: "The most basic truth is this: leadership always comes back to people. People are not in the organization, they are the organization . . . it is the people in the organization that make the difference. Nothing will ever replace the human dimension. In the end, service to nation is not about good management or technology; it is about putting our young men and women in the mud and leading them to victory."

Enlightened leaders of the new Army saw that the humane treatment of soldiers was the primary way to secure these soldiers' full cooperation with and sense of personal ownership of the Army and its mission. This may not be a new lesson for most civilian leaders, but it was a dramatic change in the way the Army did business.

It bears repeating that soldiers who are well educated, informed, and sensitive to their diversity expect to be treated with nothing less than total respect and dignity. Humane treatment is a fundamental need for the volunteer soldier. Traditional basic training methods that involved physical and emotional abuse were counterproductive and in many instances had effects that were the opposite of what was intended. These techniques reduced the soldier's ability to learn because they inhibited concentration, reduced the ability to retain information, and distracted from the task at hand. The possibility of risk taking and creative thinking was virtually eliminated. Abusive treatment made soldiers focus on avoiding being singled out and making mistakes instead of on learning. Furthermore, living and working conditions needed to be at least somewhat comparable to those of U.S. society in general. Pay needed to be improved. Training had to be more meaningful and challenging. And the bureaucratic nonsense and distractions from mission that had traditionally hamstrung the Army needed to be dramatically reduced if not eliminated. Army leadership saw these steps as essential if the AVF were to succeed and flourish.

The concern among Army traditionalists, whether on active duty or retired, was and to some degree still is that this new treatment of soldiers—caring for them and meeting their needs—would not toughen troops sufficiently for combat and that training without some personal harassment would be ineffective. In fact, just the opposite was found to be true. Soldiers' behavior during the conflicts in Grenada, Panama, and the Persian Gulf clearly indicated that more humane treatment motivated Army personnel and did not negatively affect their performance in battle. At the same time, the Army has not turned into a country club. Training still puts troops through stress, but the stress doesn't arise from degrading harassment. Rather it results from time pressures, difficult conditions, and challenging tasks involving some degree of personal risk.

Army leadership further recognized that human nature being what it is, this more enlightened treatment of soldiers and meeting of their needs has to be done in concert with other elements such as high standards of training and personal conduct, crystal-clear expectations, and equitably enforced discipline. These elements are mandatory; without them, the Army traditionalists would probably be proved right.

However, when led and trained with this combination of essential elements, the U.S. soldier has no rival in the world. Having implemented this style of *enlightened leadership*—as it is now referred to at the U.S. Military Academy—I speak from experience. During my five tours as a unit commander I found that this approach not only works but works well.

In Desert Storm and Desert Shield, I commanded a unit of six hundred paratroopers (including seventy-two women) known as the Nighthawks. These soldiers knew that their basic physiological needs would be met, that expectations would be clearly and constantly communicated, that standards of conduct and discipline would be enforced, and that they were trained and prepared to perform their mission. Morale remained high throughout the nine-month deployment as the Nighthawks successfully performed all their assigned tasks. All six hundred soldiers returned home safely.

The Gulf War experience validated for the Army's leadership a key lesson—that soldiers, as human beings, have a basic need to be accepted and treated with respect, trust, and dignity. If an organization treats individuals in this way, then the individuals will accept and take ownership of the organization's vision, values, and imperatives. If this basic need is not met, then it's questionable whether people will sign on to the other elements of the organizational culture. The Army has adopted this principle as critical to its combat effectiveness and even its very survival.

HUMAN NEEDS

In 1954, psychologist Abraham Maslow published his extensive research on human needs—work now known as the *hierarchy of needs*. Maslow's thesis is that humans have five levels of need. As one level of need is met, the individual works toward meeting the next most important level. The foundational level is physiological needs, which include such survival basics as air, water, and food. The next level is safety and security—reflecting the human desire for protection and stability. Maslow divided the third level, which includes social needs, into two parts: the need to belong to a group (affiliation) and the need for acceptance, caring, and affection.

Here is where I believe Maslow got it wrong. My experience and dissertation research indicate that what Maslow saw as the third level of need is in fact the level to which people give the highest precedence. During the Vietnam and Gulf wars, I saw soldiers give up, at least temporarily, physiological needs such as food, sleep, and shelter in order to accomplish their mission. I also saw them relinquish the need for safety and security, willingly putting themselves in harm's way, and risking death in order to retain their status in and acceptance by the group to which they belonged.

So soldiers would pass over the first two levels of need to meet the third, social level of need. The worst thing that could be said to a soldier after a firefight was, "Where were you when the chips were down?" Soldiers depend on one another for survival, and if a soldier doesn't pull his weight he jeopardizes the others in his unit. Not only that, but the soldier can be blackballed by the group, thereby threatening his own survival. In military situations, therefore, the need for belonging to the group and having its approval and respect takes precedence over Maslow's first two levels of need.

This principle has been reinforced by my experience at the Center for Creative Leadership. An assessment instrument called FIRO-B, used in most of CCL's programs, employs a questionnaire on which participants report their expressed and wanted needs in three categories: inclusion, control, and affection. Participants routinely give the highest scores to their desire for open and honest relationships. This indicates that people place the highest priority on emotional connection, open and honest communication, and close, strong relationships. It also backs up my theory that the strongest human need is the need for group acceptance, affiliation, and affection.

There is a simple yet profound leadership lesson here. If leaders help followers meet the need for affiliation, acceptance, appreciation, validation, approval, respect, and understanding, there is a high probability that the organization will achieve its mission and its vision—even, or perhaps especially, when the workforce is changing.

THE BEDROCK OF SUCCESS

The Army's handling of its changing workforce in the post-Vietnam era was guided by enlightened leadership. The Army's vision, values, imperatives, personnel selection, leadership development, and diversity—all tied together by the new appreciation for meeting basic human social needs—provide a model for civilian leaders that is filled with practical principles. Despite all the Army's success, however, it has not completed its work. Key issues—such as recruiting and retention, women in combat, and sexual harassment—remain as challenges. There is little doubt, however, that the Army's evolution into an organization whose leadership treats individuals with respect, trust, and dignity will be invaluable in meeting those challenges.

In Search of Authenticity: Now More Than Ever, Soft Skills Are Needed

Kerry Bunker and Michael Wakefield

In an environment where organizations and their people are experiencing greater and faster change—often highly disruptive change—it's crucial that more emphasis be placed on identifying and developing executives who possess emotional intelligence skills in addition to the more traditional leadership competencies. Among other things, today's leaders need to manage the dynamic tension between a *sense of urgency* and *realistic patience* and between *optimism* and *realism and openness.*

Who wants to be a leader? Today's turbulent times make this a critical question. Leading others has always been a delicate balancing act, but recent events have placed a giant exclamation point on the complexity and fragility of leadership. Foundering world economies, corporate financial scandals, recessions and downsizings, and the explosion of information technology have rocked the organizational terrain. Add to these dynamics the continuing threat of terrorism in the world, and one sees leadership challenges that are steeped in uncertainty and fraught with human and emotional concerns. Leaders face more pressure than ever to strike just the right chord with employees, colleagues, and other stakeholders.

Extraordinary times make it both more critical and more difficult to focus simultaneously on meeting the demands of managing the business and providing effective leadership to the organization's people. More often than not, it is the focus on the people side of leadership that loses out. This can be disastrous in a world where workers have experienced compounding waves of significant change—the kind of change that disrupts the foundations on which organizational systems operate. Left unattended, the fallout from such events can undermine the culture and erode the values that engender commitment. The rules on how best to serve and belong to the organization become more ambiguous. The predictability of future employment is taken away. Loyalty and trust give way to insecurity and fear, and productivity and enthusiasm are displaced by withdrawal and skepticism.

WHERE THEY ARE

In our work with organizations in transition, we have found it useful to keep the following adage in mind: "If you want to lead people somewhere new, you need to meet them where they are."

And you should not expect that people are starting out where you would prefer them to be. People's identities become entangled in their work. Thus prolonged and repeated disruptions of work threaten not only people's livelihoods and day-to-day routines but also their psychological well-being and sense of self-efficacy. The fear that results can emerge in subtle but powerful ways. People become less inclined to take the kinds of risks that will likely be required to meet extraordinary demands. They are reluctant because they fear the consequences that a mistake might bring. They develop an insatiable thirst for information that is driven more by a need for self-protection than by a desire to acquire new knowledge. They are more reticent and cautious about trusting others in general and leadership in particular. They assess the motives and intentions of leaders with a heightened sense of vigilance and skepticism. One of their goals is to read between the lines and figure out what is really going on. This self-protective behavior by humans is not unlike that by members of any other species when they feel threatened, cornered, and overwhelmed.

When people are in this state, you simply can't shake them hard enough or slap them often enough to force them onto your personal timetable for recovery and adaptability. What *is* required

---

is the skill and willingness to go back and wade into the tumultuous water *with* people and to inspire the courage and confidence they need to release their fears and reengage in the journey. Trust hangs in the balance of this commitment to meet people where they are. Without trust, not much else is possible.

RAISING THE BAR
Providing effective leadership in such an environment increasingly demands that greater emphasis be placed on identifying and developing executives who possess emotional intelligence skills in addition to the more traditional competencies in strategic and financial planning, manufacturing, team leadership, sales, and marketing. The modern leader must have the ability to understand the complex and varied impacts that difficult times have on people and to provide authentic and empathetic leadership that facilitates healing, revitalization, and commitment in others.

For seven years we worked with mid- to senior-level executives whose organizations were experiencing turbulent times and powerful transitional events. When members of these organizations were asked what they expected from their leaders during chaotic times, the answers were often paradoxical, which was reflected in the phrase *but also*. For example, people expressed a desire for leaders who are

- Courageous and committed enough to provide confidence and stability but also vulnerable enough to identify with and model an effective response to what people are going through

- Tough and inspiring enough to energize others and get them moving in the right direction but also patient enough to allow them to grieve over their losses and catch up with the transition

- Strong and self-reliant enough to take the lead and forge the way ahead but also open enough to seek input, admit mistakes, and own up to what they themselves don't know

Managing the dynamic tensions among these competing competencies can be a tall order for executives, many of whom were educated in business schools that focused primarily on the "hard" skills of management. But people today have growing expectations that executives will be equally or even more proficient in the "soft" leadership skills. For example, people count on their leaders to serve effectively as mentors, coaches, partners, counselors, team builders, allies, and champions of organizational change, and to model attributes such as honesty, integrity, energy, trust, intuition, imagination, resilience, empathy, courage, conscience, ethics, and humility—all with little developmental help or guidance. Clearly the bar has been raised for senior leadership.

OUT OF TRUE

Difficult times and constant transition trigger the need for a reframing of leadership capacities. Accepting the challenge of leading in turbulent times involves navigating between feelings and behaviors that appear oppositional and antithetical on the surface. Meeting these seemingly contradictory demands requires the ability to maintain a dynamic tension between equally important but paradoxical leadership competencies.

Imagine a bicycle wheel, with twelve spokes representing the core demands of leadership during transition and the hub representing trust. The tuning of the spokes is critical to the performance of the wheel. Do you remember what happened to your bike (and the way your bike rode) when the tension among the spokes on one of the wheels—especially spokes directly opposite each other—got out of balance? The wheel got *out of true*—it was no longer accurately fitted.

Although such tuning errors might be subtle and nearly imperceptible to the casual observer, even a brief trip around the block exposes wobbles and thumps that undermine the safety, success, and integrity of the ride. As it turns out, the same thing happens in organizations. When leaders don't effectively balance opposing leadership behaviors, both they and their organizations can become out of true. Unfortunately, these subtle flaws in the tuning of equally important leadership competencies are not readily observable to the naked eye. Experienced cyclists will tell you that you need to take a ride on a bike to determine whether a wheel is out of true, or better yet, you can spin a wheel to assess which spokes are too tight or too loose. However, more casual riders might not know enough to seek out such an assessment. After experiencing a wobbly ride they are more likely to simply hop off and conclude that they have ridden on a lousy bike. The same is true of employees under stress. They are less likely to assume that a leader might have one or two competencies that may need some fine-tuning and more likely to decide that the leader is simply incompetent overall. Indeed, they may even generalize to a higher level and conclude that the organization just doesn't have very good leadership. The bottom line is that trust is undermined and questions are raised about the personal authenticity and credibility of individual leaders. And authenticity and trust represent the core ingredients required to lead others through transition.

THE RIGHT TENSION

We want to illustrate this by focusing on two pairs of spokes that seem especially relevant in light of recent events. One pair has *sense of urgency* as a spoke on one side of the wheel of authentic leadership and *realistic patience* on the opposing side. The second pair has *optimism* on one side and *realism and openness* on the other. Maintaining the appropriate tension between these paradoxical opposites is always a subtle and fragile process. Both aspects of each pair represent important components of leadership during transition, but each is also subject to being overemphasized or underemphasized. Developing and maintaining the appropriate dynamic tension between these competing competencies becomes even more challenging during times of stress and strain.

Sense of Urgency Versus Realistic Patience

Two of a leader's primary functions during extraordinary or challenging times are to get things moving and to maintain momentum. People need to know where they stand and where they are going. They need to be challenged by stretch targets that are tough but attainable. Perhaps most important, people need to draw energy and motivation from a leader who couples confidence in their long-term prospects with a wisdom about the key steps required to get them where they want to go. This is what is meant by a *sense of urgency*.

Realistic patience is required to understand the natural emotional processes that people go through as they adapt to major change or difficult events. Demonstrating such patience involves explaining the why and the how of what needs to be done, coaching people who are struggling, restating important messages, listening, and understanding that performance may initially lag as people acquire new skills.

When this pair of competencies is out of true, the resulting behavior usually takes the form of overdoing the sense of urgency while underdoing or ignoring the process that others must go through to recover and adapt. Leaders need to remember that they typically have the benefit of a head start in accepting the transition process because they have more lead time, more information, and more control over the situation. A common mistake is to push too hard when the change is fresh and the future direction is still unclear. As paradoxical as it sounds, having patience with people and allowing the new dynamic to unfold more naturally ultimately lets the organization gain momentum and energy and move faster. People can see through activity for the sake of activity. Attempts to make everything an urgent priority simply undermine the credibility of leadership and cause others to become discouraged, disengaged, and cynical. A leader's failure to understand the source of these emotional reactions only reinforces people's notion that leadership is insensitive and out of touch.

Howard Lutnick, chairman and CEO of financial services firm Cantor Fitzgerald, wrestled publicly with the balance between these competing needs in the aftermath of the September 11, 2001, attacks on the World Trade Center, which took a huge toll on his organization—more than 700 employees were killed. He grieved openly about the loss of his firm's people and expressed his compassion and understanding for all the others deeply affected by this loss. He vowed to find a way to take care of surviving family members. At the same time he recognized that time was of the essence in getting his organization up and running again. Failure to do so would have made his other promise impossible to fulfill. He appears to have succeeded at both his objectives, but along the way he was buffeted by the emotional reactions that his people and the media had to each step in the process. His well-intentioned though rocky journey highlights how difficult it is to use just the right amounts of these opposing competencies in a stress-laden environment.

Optimism Versus Realism and Openness

Optimism is seeing the glass as half full and being determined and resolute. This involves offering inspiring projections of what the future holds and generating a contagious level of energy, enthusiasm, and confidence about what can be achieved. There is no question that optimism is a characteristic that is correlated with success not only in leadership but also in life.

However, research on learning and resiliency suggests that optimism must be tempered by reality, reason, and rationality if it is to have maximum effect. Optimism unchecked by common sense and reason can lead to a dangerous form of cluelessness and "blowing smoke." Leaders get themselves in trouble when they are optimistically blind to the flaws in their plans and unwilling to own up to their miscalculations and mistakes. In their sincere efforts to be courageous and upbeat, leaders must not forget that people also expect them to be realistic, honest, authentic, and forthright.

Genuine *realism and openness* means being truthful and candid even when it hurts to do so. It's being resolute and hopeful without resorting to sugarcoating, deception, or minimizing what the leader doesn't know. When leaders overdo optimism, people think they're not in touch with reality. They are perceived as spin-meisters or operators. When this happens, people can get stuck in a state of resistance and become passive-aggressive.

TAKING THE RISKS

In general the leaders we have worked with are extraordinarily bright and talented. Most have a conceptual understanding of the emotional impact that difficult times have on organizations and the people in them. They can speak to the need for empathy and articulate all the right words about people being the organization's most important asset. But the ultimate test lies in bringing these softer skills to life when confronted with challenges that trigger instinctive tendencies on the opposite side of the wheel. In times of stress it is natural to fall back on one's strengths, which for most executives reside in the more traditional leadership and management competencies. Becoming adept at the emotional and relational competencies is riskier and more difficult because it requires that leaders go inside themselves to get in touch with their own human reactions. Modeling effective recovery and adaptation requires having the capacity to make the journey first yourself. Such learning doesn't come naturally or easily at first, but it is the key to becoming more effective during transitions. Based on what we have seen, leaders can benefit greatly from coaching and experiential learning events designed to provide "deep dives" into the emotional aspects of bouncing back from change and transition.

People at CCL feel they are beginning to understand a lot about the competing demands of leadership in difficult times. Although they don't profess to have solutions for all the dilemmas that emerge, they are developing an increasingly clear picture of what effective leadership might look like during such times. And they can use that framework to continue to develop approaches that help leaders "true up" the dynamic tensions between opposing spokes. In the end this is not something a leader can fake. The essence of authentic leadership emerges when leaders feel safe in expressing who they are as people.

Former New York City Mayor Rudolph Giuliani, asked by a reporter how he knew what to do in the aftermath of the September 11 attacks, had an insightful response: "Nobody knew what to do. You had to act on instinct." There is a great lesson in that answer for every leader. Leaders should put aside their notions of how leaders are supposed to act and be more authentic as people. That's the first and most important step.

The Luxury of Tough Times: Five Terrific Questions

Keir Carroll

Few people would claim that *tough times*—times of great upheaval, economic or otherwise—are better (or better for us) than *good times*. Who, after all, would disagree with British author Kingsley Amis's classic understatement: "There was no end to the ways in which nice things are nicer than nasty ones." Or with the great singer and comedian Sophie Tucker's emphatic assertion: "I've been rich and I've been poor. Believe me, honey, rich is better."

But I would make the claim that tough times—times when great change and anxiety often freeze us in suspended animation—can provide a certain luxury: the luxury of reflection and insight.

In good times it is easy to whirl around in the blender of daily life in blameless busyness, staying a step ahead of the blades, in the puree, in a frenzy of doing, doing, doing. We pack our days with e-mail wars and worthless meetings, constantly responding to low-value requests in order to stave off sneer pressure and constantly complaining that we never have enough time to think, reflect, or plan. Anyone who cries out, "Stop the madness!" is branded a troublemaker. Anyone who says, "Don't just do something—sit there!" is labeled a lunatic. Anyone caught staring at the ceiling, reflecting on what *has* been and what *needs to be*, is simply a slacker.

It is much more comfortable living down in the blender than up in the helicopter. Spinning around with everyone else is a form of mass hysteria after all—we agree to believe that we are doing the right things together. We may be exhausted but we are exhausted together. We may be frustrated but we are frustrated together. We may be angry but we are angry together. And when we succeed, if we have time, we can celebrate together.

Tough times, in contrast, can boot us out of the blender and into the helicopter. The stomach lurches, the heart pounds, and we are terrified and exhilarated all at one time. We are smacked awake. Up in the helicopter, above the whirling and whimpering, we are granted the luxury of confronting the tough questions we know we really should have been asking when times were good.

It's lonely up there. We lose the comfort of busyness. Instead, our primary job is to see life steady and see it whole: to assess paths taken and not taken and catalogue our organization's and our own sins of omission and commission, the weaknesses, blind spots, follies, and fears that are too uncomfortable to face let alone name out loud. It's hard work. It can feel overwhelming. But it is noble work, and it is indispensable for future success.

Usually it takes a near-death experience to jolt us into facing the big questions—questions like *Who am I? What do I stand for? How do I want to be remembered?* Talk to anyone who has struggled—often in a hospital bed—through the dark night of the soul and emerged into the sunshine, and what will often strike you is his or her renewed zest for life, serenity, solidity, and ability to look reality straight in the eye.

These individuals see themselves not as being cursed with a catastrophe but as being blessed with a priceless opportunity: the opportunity to put themselves in perspective.

FINDING HIMSELF

Here's a case in point: Robert from Scotland, a workaholic; task-addicted and hard-driving; the embodiment of the ambitious, up-and-coming manager; fired with adrenaline; neglectful of his young family. His heart attack at a ludicrously young age propelled him on a six-month journey of self-discovery. He brought what he discovered back to his team. His discovery was in many ways mundane: "I am a person," he said in his fierce and almost impenetrable Scottish accent, "who cares about achieving superlative results and cares about being with the people I love, and the two need not be mutually exclusive." He and his team became ruthless in uncluttering their work lives. If a task was merely urgent but unimportant to the present or future success of the business, it was kicked off the list. If a meeting was merely a ritual blamestorming session, it was kicked off the calendar. If it was five thirty, then it was time to go home. Period.

The result? Clarity of purpose. Focus. Results! Energy and passion and a life lived not on the fringes of BlackBerrying but in joyful bites. What courage it took to insist on doing only important work! Talking with Robert was humbling. Hearing others talk *about* Robert was inspiring.

Tough times simulate that opportunity. We can choose to hunker in the bunker, terrified to take any action for fear of making a mistake, cc-ing the world to cover our rear ends. We can choose to redouble our efforts, doing the same things over and over again in the vain hope that we will get different results. Or we can choose to see this time as an opportunity to take stock, get clear on what matters and what doesn't, and find the wellspring of strength necessary to create or profit from the good times again.

ASKING OURSELVES

So in tough times, there are five terrific questions we can ask. The first is *What are we all about?* In other words, do we have a core or are we all mirror? What are the values we have been living, not merely espousing? Are we like those Wall Street giants whose lived values seem to have been "line my pockets and stay out of jail"? Have our choices been selfish and expedient, or have we struggled to mean something through our actions? Wherever we are in the organization, what code or principles do we try to embody?

Sometimes those principles are lofty indeed. Sometimes they are earthy. A great favorite of mine came from a senior executive of a multinational insurance company in his address to managers during a workshop: "If you're not developing people and

you're not having fun, then all you have left is—good grief!—
insurance!"

The second terrific question: *How have we thought of
ourselves as leaders?* Put in other terms, have we subscribed to the
big brain theory, jealously keeping to ourselves the right to think
and experiment and decide what needs to be done? Or have we
been quick to involve the intelligence and imagination and vigor
of those around us? In the best of times these are hard questions
because they oblige us to test our *actions* (do we actually adopt
opposing ideas?) against our *lip service* (we know it's important
to listen!). What about now, in what feels like the worst of times?
Tough times tempt us to retrench, batten down the hatches, and
fear losing control over circumstances—and thus to shut out and
shut down the very people whose energy and commitment we
most need. Tough times, then, test our honesty: Are we living the
leadership legend we believe we are?

The third terrific question: *How have we thought of our followers?* Take Sally, a wonderful manager, highly respected, quickly
promoted, a star. Her philosophy: "People are grown-ups. Not all
of them realize it. My job is to help them realize it." When she
took over management of a struggling team, she sat down once
a week with each team member individually and asked him or
her—very gently—four questions:

- What's going well?

- What's not going well?

- What are you doing about what's not going well?

- What support do you need from me?

At first, the meetings were very brief. It took time for trust
to develop. Then, suddenly, the meetings seemed to take forever
as individuals not only unburdened themselves of their workplace frustrations but also gloried in the challenge of imagining
solutions. After a surprisingly short time, the meetings were very

brief again as people realized they had been licensed by the third question to think for themselves, reach out to teammates, and take responsibility for solving their own problems. As a result, the team became close-knit, high-performing, self-reliant, and proud of its successes.

Now, in tough times, Sally has a real dilemma. Is her job to protect her team from harsh realities, to give them, like a caring parent, reassuring and optimistic answers to their fearful questions? Or does she come clean, confess her own uncertainty and insecurity, and invite them to join her in working through unpredictable difficulties toward uncertain success? In other words, are they grown-up *enough* yet?

Sally is smart and emotionally acute. There is no doubt she will figure out where on the spectrum from extreme optimism to utter pessimism she needs to be to keep her team ready for the good times to come. The point is that she is asking herself the right questions and knows her team well enough to make a smart choice.

The fourth terrific question: *How are we building the team of the future?* When good times return, will we be ready for them? Will we have the right people in place, with the right skills and spirit so that we are already on the starting blocks, ready to leave our competition in the dust?

This is a tough set of questions even in good times. Organizations love to make people repeat themselves. My own work history provides a case in point. In the early 1980s, despite ludicrous odds, my team at an eminent Harvard University–affiliated teaching hospital had managed to pull off a special project without authority, budget, clout, or willing cooperation from powerful forces. Another similar effort was on the horizon, and, naturally, the organization came to me, eager to have me repeat the success. And I, of course, was eager to prove that the first project had not been merely a fluke and that I was, in fact, much smarter than I looked. Luckily, Art Stomberg, the hospital's vice president of planning and my mentor and boss, warned me off. "Look," he said, shaking his head like a puzzled bear. "Why do you think I sent *you* over to MIT to work on that task force? Why do you think I had *you* do all the presentations in the auditorium in front of those ugly, angry mobs? Why did I send *you* to represent us at those conventions? Why am I having *you* help me reallocate the million or so square feet of space we now have? Not so you could repeat yourself! No! I did it all so you'd be ready for bigger and better things!" And of course, he was right. An untutored genius when it came to mentoring, Stomberg dedicated himself to building talent for the future. When you worked for him, he gave you opportunities to sample the tasks necessary for the next stage in your career. His daily question—"So when are you leaving?!"— was a constant reminder to look forward and be ready.

In tough times, the temptation to do the opposite is overwhelming. Case in point: a favorite client reports that her boss is no longer her boss. No, she's been asked to go back to her previous role and make the unit shipshape again. And her boss's boss has been asked to go back and tidy up *her* old unit too. Neither one of them will be doing anything new. They will be learning nothing new. They will be bored out of their minds.

And those in the units right now, looking to stretch and learn? They are blocked, denied a stimulating challenge, and likewise condemned to repetition. It's what a colleague of mine calls a WOMBAT: a waste of money, brains, and talent.

The fifth and final terrific question: *What will be our legacy?* In other words, what is the future we want to look back on? Few of us will have the legacy of Christopher Wren, architect of London's St. Paul's Cathedral, where he is buried. A plain plaque in Latin reads, more or less, "If you are seeking a monument to his memory, just look around you." At the other extreme, there is the wonderfully sardonic *New Yorker* cartoon showing a stoop-shouldered elderly widow, bedraggled bouquet in hand, staring at her husband's simple epitaph: "He watched sports." It's quite a spectrum.

When we are clinging to the side of the planet by our fingernails, waiting for the next round of layoffs, our legacy is probably the last thing on our minds. Instead we are seduced into the thickets of politicking and rumor-hunting. Or we are frozen by anxiety. Or we are hounded by self-doubt. Or we wrap ourselves in a cloak of magical thinking.

What if, instead, we were to ask ourselves, "What small action can we take today that will build a glorious future for the organization?"

Sometimes the answers are fiendishly difficult to come by. Sometimes the answers are humble or obvious: perhaps we could go talent hunting *now* so that we have the best-in-the-business bench when the world turns; perhaps we could sniff out complementary start-up businesses *now* so that we are ready to scoop them up when we have the cash; maybe we could start sounding like a global company, with our staff learning a new language *now*.

Perhaps these ideas do not sound grandiose enough. But what they really represent is a way of thinking: the habit of looking for concrete things to do *now* to be ready for the future. Typically, these things are *not* urgent, *not* on the to-do list, *not* assigned to us. They are the smart moves that occasionally cross our minds but get lost or neglected in the daily whirl of the good-times blender. Tough times provide the perfect opportunity to start building legacies, while others are immobilized by fear or suspense.

Lasting legacies need not be tangible, of course. On the contrary, it is often the intangible legacies that endure—not monuments but mind-sets. When we think of the great companies, isn't it often their passionate mind-sets that impress us? They live by their mantras: abhor waste, respond to every problem by sundown, guarantee lifetime satisfaction or your money back, and love your customers. Each mantra is someone's monument; it did not spring from nowhere.

JUST IN TIME

Remember Robert, the Scottish manager who discovered that it was possible to get spectacular results at work and have a family life too? Here's another thing he said: "Why didn't I have the brains to ask myself the important questions until it was almost too late?" Well, Robert, it's because you're only human. Better late than never.

Wired to Inspire: Leading Organizations Through Adversity

Meena S. Wilson and Susan S. Rice

Times of adversity often give rise to unpredictability, fear, anxiety, and loss of confidence. Such circumstances call for inspirational leadership, which gives employees the motivation, commitment, and productivity to take advantage of the opportunities lying on the other side of what seems to be a dark curtain of misfortune.

A software developer with an established product and a history of profitability has to deal with the bursting of the dot-com bubble and the collapse of the telecommunications market. A national textile industry trade association, contending with bankruptcies, consolidations, and plant closings among its members because of foreign competition, faces a downsizing. A global insurance company, buffeted by burgeoning worldwide terrorism, and runaway costs from class-action and asbestos lawsuit awards, must reassess its stands on risk management, underwriting discipline, and investments to maintain its status as a company that can meet its financial commitments. Skyrocketing fuel prices are having a profound effect on an interstate trucking company's bottom line. A national auto repair chain, presented with evidence that economic and demographic changes in the marketplace as well as the increased reliability of late-model vehicles are responsible for the slowdown in its business, must bank its future on something other than hoping everything will return to the way it was. A farming conglomerate, its grain production reduced by floods, hail, and wind and its deficiency payments from the U.S. Department of

Agriculture about to be reduced, needs to figure out a way to tighten its cash-flow requirements and return to profitability. The economic development board of a small country in Asia that has finite natural resources and a limited domestic market must find a way to create jobs and raise the standard of living for the nation's citizens.

It seems that today's organizations, across every industry and even among the ranks of nonprofits and government agencies, are operating in an environment that can be characterized in one word: *adversity*. Between the extremes of *stability* (which can cause leaders to become complacent) and *crisis* (which requires leaders to demonstrate heroism and sacrifice) lies *adversity*, which, as we shall see, calls for a new and different type of leadership.

Simply put, adversity is an unfortunate circumstance or event (or set of circumstances or events) that causes hardship, distress, turbulence, and uncertainty. Examples of circumstances or events that create adverse conditions are declining stock prices, a need to downsize, negative publicity, intense competition, stalled negotiations, and an inability to innovate. Adverse conditions can affect an organization in ways such as these:

- The future of the organization—and of the people in the organization—becomes increasingly unpredictable.

- Fears arise about the organization's ability to continue delivering quality products or services, maintain demand for those products or services, retain its stature and reputation in its industry and in the community, and keep up professional standards of work. Ultimately, the organization's very existence comes into doubt, and the security of employees is highly questionable. Stress levels rise.

- As doubts and anxiety erode confidence, the organization faces the possibility of falling into a downward spiral. Attention to complex tasks deteriorates, which negatively affects productivity, which in turn raises further doubts about the organization's future.

OPPORTUNITY KNOCKS

As bad as adversity can appear to be when an organization is experiencing it, there can be a silver lining. "Difficulties mastered are opportunities won," Winston Churchill said. In other words, organizations can emerge from adversity stronger than they were before, revitalized, and more resilient, mature, focused, and disciplined. New ventures and new approaches to leadership can result in a workforce that is more motivated, committed, and productive. The organization can wind up in a position to thrive rather than merely survive.

But steering an organization skillfully through adverse conditions doesn't just happen. Handling the tangibles—instituting more efficient processes, developing a strategic plan, tightening spending, diversifying the customer base, and so on—is in many ways the easy part. The trickier part is mastering the intangibles involved in practicing a model of leadership that is often qualitatively different from and runs counter to the theories of leadership prevalent in modern organizations and in society as a whole. This model is *inspirational leadership*—displaying the skills that enable leaders to motivate, grow, and build confidence in the people they lead so the organization can regularly achieve high standards of performance, even in tough times.

As people in organizations experience higher than usual levels of stress, new demands are made on their leaders. And as the work of these leaders changes, certain leadership capabilities and characteristics take on increasingly important roles:

Strategic orientation and vision. In times of adversity, it is no longer business as usual. Such times require leaders with impressive mental, social, physical, and spiritual intelligence—leaders who can see beyond the horizon and who are willing to take calculated risks. These kinds of leaders are naturally compelling as individuals. They are skilled at communicating their strategy and vision, instilling passion and confidence in those they lead, creating an environment in which people feel good about themselves and their work, acting as agents of positive change, and igniting creativity and innovation.

Perspectives and behaviors. As people in organizations look for cues on how to deal with misfortune and distress, they turn to their leaders' words and actions for inspiration and for an example they can follow. Most of the time, people are oblivious to the effects their words and actions have on others. In times of adversity, however, leaders must be aware that even their smallest gestures and comments will be scrutinized, so they must choose them well.

Sense-making communications. People operating under adverse conditions want to believe that they can negotiate their way forward and get past the unfortunate events or circumstances in a sensible way. They want to know the goals the organization will pursue and why those goals have been chosen. They also want to know what adjustments will need to be made to achieve those goals under the changed circumstances. For leaders, constructing collective intelligence through collaborative learning that helps the organization prevail over the adverse conditions becomes critical.

Competence-building communications. Employees must receive the support they need to continue performing routine tasks competently and logically and to maintain momentum through the adverse conditions. People experiencing stress need to engage with one another to bolster their sense of capability. Leaders can support their followers by taking an interest in developing them, helping them reach their full potential, and making them feel important and valued. The best way for leaders to instill competence among their subordinates is to assume responsibility for doing so.

According to social scientists, inspirational leadership surfaces naturally in response to times of uncertainty and complexity, such as these:

- During certain phases of organizational life—including the start-up stage, periods of rapid growth, and crisis situations

- During work activities that require constant adaptation, spanning boundaries, and coordinated group-based efforts
- During periods of social turbulence resulting from political or religious conflict or crisis

The unstable environment that typifies these situations is also rich in emerging or unexploited opportunities, even though the path ahead cannot be seen; there are few cues about how to proceed, and those that exist are vague; there is no formal structure for moving forward; and conventional actions are unlikely to work. Under such conditions, special effort and commitment are needed to make progress.

SECOND WIND

One of the original definitions of the word *inspire* was "to breathe life into." Inspirational leadership can breathe the capacity for responding to adversity into the heart and soul of an organization, and this capacity becomes part of the organization's culture. If people are involved in building and accomplishing the inspirational leader's vision for the organization, if their work is connected to that vision and to their own motivations and values, the value of the resulting commitment to the overall success of the organization cannot be overstated. If the organization's culture is one that inspires rather than oppresses, it can only have the effect of creating a more productive organization and profitable bottom line.

But what does inspirational leadership look like in the real world? One example is found in the results of research that CCL conducted (see the sidebar on page 98) with a governmental agency in Singapore, where CCL opened an Asian campus in February 2004.

In 1961, the Singapore Economic Development Board (EDB) was tasked with creating jobs, raising the standard of living, and carrying out other economic development efforts on behalf of this small city-state in Southeast Asia. At that time Singapore was buffeted by adverse and turbulent conditions,

A History of Inspiration

Beginning in 2000 and ending in 2002, CCL conducted a study focusing on the organizational leadership of the Singapore Economic Development Board, which is tasked with creating jobs, raising the standard of living, and other economic development efforts in this small city-state in Southeast Asia.

A proven methodology was used to take diagnostic snapshots of the leadership development needs of the organization. A representative sample of the organization's current, former, and emerging leaders was interviewed and asked to complete assessment instruments. The fifty interviewees included fifteen former leaders, seventeen current leaders (with eight to thirty-three years of experience), and eighteen emerging leaders (with one to nine years of experience). The interviews, which averaged ninety minutes in length, were done in the fall of 2000 and the spring of 2001. Seventy-four percent of the research subjects also completed the SYMLOG (System for the Multiple-Level Observation of Groups) assessment instrument, which measures current and optimal individual and organizational values and current and most-effective interpersonal behaviors.

Findings were further validated using focus-group sessions at four other governmental agencies that faced adverse and turbulent conditions similar to those experienced by the EDB. The findings were also cross-compared with results from two separate, external studies to assess the Economic Value Added realized by the EDB's customers and clients.

including extremely limited natural resources and a small market. (The secession of Singapore from Malaysia in 1965 resulted in the loss of a vast area from which to draw raw materials and of a large domestic market to absorb finished goods.) When Singapore gained independence from the United Kingdom, also in 1965, the country's labor force was largely unskilled and undereducated; the annual per capita income was US$435. The EDB was asked to stimulate the growth of Singapore's economy, with the objective of positioning Singapore as an international business center.

Persuading companies to locate in Singapore was a daunting challenge, however. The agency's officers repeatedly encountered skepticism about the business sense of placing subsidiaries in Singapore. But by scanning the international marketplace for client companies, persistently engaging those companies in conversations about Singapore's global business strategy, and painting a picture of an alluring future, the EDB contributed to Singapore's remarkably rapid transformation from a Third World entrepôt to a highly developed First World country.

The conditions under which the agency operates continue to pose obstacles and threats. China and India have become low-cost manufacturing centers. The double-digit economic growth that Singapore has experienced for much of its existence is no longer possible because the country's economy is now on a par with those of the world's most developed nations. Fundamental cultural changes are needed if Singapore's economy is to become more knowledge and innovation based.

As is the case with many organizations operating in a global marketplace, the EDB also faces numerous operational challenges: a highly competitive business environment; increased work volume, speed, and complexity; unstable client relationships and ambiguous partnering relationships; issues related to talent recruitment, development, and retention; and the complexity of integrating internally across hierarchical levels and functions.

To fulfill its mission, the EDB since its inception has needed employees who can thrive in a climate of adversity. Generations of leaders have modeled for employees the attitudes and behaviors needed to cope with adversity. Over a period spanning four decades, the agency has successfully managed to overcome the threats to economic development faced by Singapore. The EDB's leaders have inspired the agency's employees to the extent that the employees in turn have been receptive to watching and learning from the leaders' examples. The leaders have taught—and the employees have learned—how the organization can collectively respond to adversity.

The resulting resonance between leaders and followers has helped to build the organizational capacity to deal with continual but varied adverse conditions. Inspirational leadership has become part of the organization's cultural code.

EAST AND WEST

CCL's research found that the distinctive aspects of inspirational leadership at the EDB could be explained in terms of both North American leadership concepts and Asian traditions.

From a North American perspective, inspirational leadership blends the *charismatic, transformational,* and *value-based* styles of leading.

- Charismatic leaders bring unique gifts to their organization. They are visionary and have a highly developed sense of strategic timing. They are unconventional and willing to take calculated risks.

- Transformational leaders develop special relationships with their followers. They challenge the status quo and pay attention to their followers' desires to find meaning in work and for personal development.

- Value-based leaders make the daily work of their followers more meaningful. They help their organizations develop an appealing vision of what lies in the future and generate confidence that the vision can be achieved.

When these leadership styles are combined into inspirational leadership, it creates an unusually strong commitment to organization- and society-based outcomes and to innovation. In response, employees become bold, tenacious, passionate, and highly results oriented.

One example of how this model of inspirational leadership has manifested itself at the EDB is found in the agency's recent efforts to win over a global electronic manufacturing conglomerate that did not intend to locate its new plant in Singapore. Undeterred, EDB employees worked tirelessly to develop strategies to attract the attention of the conglomerate's senior executives. Many attempts were made to position Singapore and its amenities as the best choice. The deal was finally clinched when the conglomerate's executives saw the willingness of the EDB employees to arrange site visits despite the fact it was a major national holiday.

How do inspirational leaders elicit such commitment and performance even in times of adversity? The comments of the EDB leaders who participated in the CCL research are telling. "You must mobilize [employees] with something that captures their imagination, inspires them, gives them something to work with that is worthy of achieving," said one. Said another, "The work [employees] are doing must have greater meaning in the national sense rather than just personal gain and development."

Several of the EDB's founding executives were highly regarded for their vision and other leadership gifts. One was considered an excellent strategist, while another was a superb salesman and negotiator, and yet another demonstrated sound entrepreneurial instincts combined with dedication to building trust-based international networks.

The ability of inspirational leadership to animate followers into believing they can negotiate and collaborate their way past adversity is apparent in another example of an EDB success story. In 1997, when Singapore slipped into a recession along with the rest of the region, the EDB quickly set up several task forces.

Each task force was divided into subgroups, and each subgroup held twenty to thirty meetings with CEOs and chairpersons of private and public sector organizations. The findings were compiled into a competitiveness report that outlined what Singapore would have to do to reengineer its economy. This resulted in the current thrust toward a knowledge-based economy, which has been highly successful.

ROLE MODELS

From an Asian perspective, inspirational leadership is marked by paternalism and human-heartedness. Paternalistic, human-hearted leaders are kind to and respect their followers. They believe that the welfare of the group and society depends on their exercising a beneficial, moral influence. This is achieved by being role models and teachers who show restraint and benevolence.

Paternalism and human-heartedness are more common in cultures that have a group orientation, particularly those in which age and other forms of hierarchical status are respected. Another manifestation of paternalism and human-heartedness consists of the formal and informal teaching-learning relationships that naturally form between senior and junior employees. An apprenticeship system based on synergistic relationships is developed, as veterans with experience are willing to teach and newcomers with initiative are interested in learning and succeeding.

A prime example of how this dynamic plays out at the EDB is Chan Chin Bock, a former EDB chairman who was the first officer of the agency to be posted to the United States to get U.S. companies to invest in Singapore. Chan eventually set up EDB offices in thirteen cities worldwide—including those in Chicago, London, Frankfurt, and Zurich. In an article in Singapore's *Straits Times,* Chan related how his greatest satisfaction comes from watching the many EDB protégés he has nurtured go on to succeed. CCL learned from its research that this high level of involvement with the professional and personal development of employees has been typical of the EDB's senior leaders throughout the agency's existence.

Another aspect of the Asian perspective on inspirational leadership is reaffirmation of the moral basis of people's obligations to one another during times of adversity. Although setbacks need to be acknowledged, at the same time extra effort must be invoked and mobilized. At a recent meeting between an executive of the EDB and representatives of another Singaporean governmental agency, for instance, the EDB executive discerned that the leaders of the other agency were interested in developing their organization's capacity for promoting investment in Singapore. Sharing the EDB's expertise in this area with the other agency was an important step in building a mutually beneficial relationship between the two organizations.

GAINING AN EDGE

When inspirational leadership is practiced effectively, a clanlike culture develops in the organization. The leadership's vision and values are internalized. Followers learn which goals to value and how to achieve these goals by following logical administrative processes. They willingly demonstrate their own capacity for leading with inspiration and develop deep and productive relationships with colleagues at all levels. The organization is able to capitalize on the opportunities that are inherent in adversity and in so doing acquires considerable influence and impact—and the competitive edge that is so important in today's business environment.

After the Storm: Leading in the Wake of a Crisis

Gene Klann

A lot has been said and written about what leaders need to do during a crisis and to prepare for a crisis. But leadership in the period *after* a crisis has drawn less attention, even though it may be just as important for an organization's viability. Here's a primer to help leaders enable their organizations to emerge from a crisis not only intact but stronger and more purposeful.

The period from September 11, 2001, through the end of 2002 provided many unwelcome opportunities to learn how to be an effective leader during a crisis. The attacks on the World Trade Center and the Pentagon on 9/11 left the leaders of the companies and military departments that occupied those buildings in a state of shock. They struggled to cope with the devastating loss of life suffered by their organizations and somehow regroup and carry on. Soon after, a series of exposures to anthrax spores delivered through the mail resulted in the deaths of four workers and tested the resilience of the leadership of the U.S. Postal Service as well as the media organizations and governmental offices that had been targeted. Then a nonlethal but still chaos-inducing crisis emerged as a procession of companies was linked to accounting and fraud scandals of mammoth proportions, sending the offending organizations into free fall and America's trust in corporate leadership into the tank. And finally, a sniper spree cast a pall of terror and anxiety over the Washington, D.C., region for three weeks as law enforcement, governmental, and school officials tried to infuse perseverance, hope, and calm through their leadership.

In each case the effectiveness of the leaders embroiled in the crisis was sometimes crystal clear, sometimes painfully lacking or

even nonexistent. But much was learned about providing leadership during a crisis, and a consensus emerged that good leaders
naturally and rightfully turn their attention to the human side of

the crisis—to the emotional and physical needs and concerns of their followers. A crisis can strike any company at any time, and there are many eventualities aside from the types of crises seen in the recent past that can land organizations in trouble—financial catastrophes; problems that threaten the public image of a company or product; and disasters that pose a danger to consumers, employees, the community, or the environment.

In any such event the three key approaches for leaders are to communicate fully and honestly; to set an example of consistency; and to be present, visible, and totally involved in the situation and attempts to mitigate it. In these ways leaders can offer those they lead constructive means for dealing with fear, stress, grief, and anxiety; for maintaining focus and productivity; and for picking themselves up and moving forward with renewed strength.

BUILDING TO LAST

But what happens after a crisis is over? Are there steps leaders can take to ensure that the organization and its employees establish a daily routine that does not passively fall back on practices that during the crisis were found to feed uncertainty, fear, panic, and a lack of trust but instead builds on new insights, strengths, responsibilities, and cooperation to enhance cohesion, balance, focus, productivity, and readiness to meet challenges? The goal of leadership after a crisis is to rebuild and strengthen relationships and to learn from the experience to be better prepared for any future crisis. Leaders who view the period of recovery after a crisis as an opportunity and an impetus to develop a better routine can help their organizations emerge stronger and more purposeful.

The first challenge for leaders is more difficult than it may sound: recognizing when the crisis has passed. A crisis may end, but it doesn't just fade away; the ensuing period of repair, recovery, and healing is likely to be long term, difficult, and painful—physically, emotionally, and financially. However, a number of signs can help leaders recognize when the immediate crisis is over:

- The news media have dropped coverage of the story or are no longer giving it high visibility.

- The organization and its employees are slowly returning to something approaching normalcy.

- The number of inquiries about the crisis from outside the organization—from customers, suppliers, shareholders, the community, and employees' families, for instance—has dropped considerably.

- Internal rumors and employees' anxiety levels have returned to normal.

One of the most important things for leaders to do after a crisis is to assure employees that the likelihood of an identical crisis occurring is very low. This reduces employees' anxiety and increases their morale and productivity. Leaders can accomplish this in a number of ways. First, they should talk with the employees personally and be open to questions; this behavior can have a therapeutic and calming effect. Second, leaders should oversee a comprehensive update of company operations, rules, and regulations, with the aim of preventing a similar crisis, and should share these measures with the employees. The update can address improved crisis assessment procedures, including those designed for early warning and detection, and better methods of communication among leaders and employees. The latter deserve special attention. Just as clear and continuing communication is essential to preparing for a crisis and leading during a crisis, keeping the lines of communication open and reviewing and rebuilding the organization's communication strategies after a crisis helps the organization and everyone in it learn from the experience and be better able to deal effectively with any future crisis.

CAUSES AND EFFECTS

One of the biggest challenges for leaders after a crisis is determining all the causes of the crisis. If this is not done or not done well, the likelihood of the crisis reoccurring increases.

Determining all the causes and effects of a crisis and informing employees of the findings are key to bolstering the employees' emotions and behavior and the organization's recovery overall. When a crisis is over, people naturally want to know what happened, why it happened, what it means for them and for the organization, and what is being done to make sure it won't happen again.

A crisis seldom has a single cause, and finding out all the causes requires good and complete information, diligent research, and intuitive thinking. It also requires consulting every source of information, no matter how seemingly insignificant or unrelated. Sources may include customer feedback, production reports, safety data, and employee complaints and suggestions. The information-gathering process should begin as soon as possible after the crisis is contained.

Similarly, leaders should closely scrutinize the effects of the crisis. Some effects will be plainly evident in the immediate aftermath of the crisis, but it's highly likely that other effects will emerge as time passes and the dust settles—and the effects that are at first hidden may have even more severe consequences than the primary effects. Secondary effects may include financial costs, emotional consequences, and fallout from the community.

Leaders should review how they, their employees, and the organization overall reacted during the crisis and any lingering effects. The best way to begin this review is to assess the emotional state of the workforce. Some employees will still be emotionally distressed, and leaders need to address these employees' needs and find ways to help them cope with their fear, pain, and stress.

One way for leaders to do this is simply to walk around, listen to employees, and be available to offer encouragement and support. This personal approach not only strengthens communication lines but also builds the relationships that are essential to dealing effectively with any future crisis. Leaders should also consider making counseling available and endorsing and underwriting support and discussion groups that could meet during working hours.

Next, leaders should review how the organization overall reacted during the crisis. One way to do this is through a process similar to the U.S. Army's After Action Review. Previous attempts by corporations to assimilate this process have met with mixed success. The key is to treat the crisis review process not as a one-time postmortem but as an ongoing organizational learning practice and a disciplined approach to improving performance over time.

During the crisis review process the people who were most closely involved in the crisis record their impressions and recollections of the organization's response to the crisis—what went well and what didn't go well or could have gone better. Looking at the bigger picture, the review participants should determine not only what was learned but also when and how the organization will apply what was learned. The crisis review can be carried out by a large group or by several smaller groups; in the Army's experience, smaller groups work best because reviewers are more likely to share sensitive information in small groups than in large groups.

The information and conclusions gathered during a crisis review can be grouped into two categories: *validations* and *lessons learned*. The former are reinforcements of the things that worked well; the latter are reflections on the things that didn't work well or that the organization did not do but should have done.

A crisis review should not be intended to cast blame or to find and penalize anyone who may have had a hand in creating the crisis or in failing to react to it appropriately. The main focus of a crisis review should be to learn from the crisis—not to determine responsibility, accountability, or guilt. If an organization is inclined to determine who, if anyone, was responsible for the crisis, it should undertake additional procedures separate from the crisis review, such as a formal internal inquiry or an outside legal action. For some crises, determining who was responsible and bringing the guilty party or parties to justice is not only appropriate but mandatory because it may be the only way for employees and others who feel they have been victimized by the culpable individual or individuals to heal.

CALL TO ACTION

The next step for leaders after a crisis is to incorporate the findings of the crisis review into an organizational crisis action plan. Again, special emphasis should be placed on communication before, during, and after the crisis. The lessons drawn from the crisis review can be used to update and improve the organization's crisis communication tactics, such as responding quickly when a disaster occurs, managing the organization's messages during a crisis, establishing a policy for dealing with the media, monitoring news coverage, and defining how and to whom employees should report a potential crisis situation.

The information and lessons unearthed during the crisis review process can also be used to draw up the what-if scenarios that are part of an effective crisis action plan and to write the final organizational report on the crisis. Employees should be briefed on the report and trained on how the crisis action plan works and their role in it; these steps not only fulfill the requisite of communication but also boost employees' confidence in their leadership as they see that crisis prevention and planning are priorities.

Aside from the crisis action plan, leaders should eliminate or change organizational procedures, policies, and regulations that were found to be inadequate during the crisis.

VALUES ADDED

Additional elements that leaders should review and revise after a crisis are the organization's vision and values. How did they fare during the crisis? Did they help or hinder the organization in weathering the storm? Did the organization and its leaders live up to their values during the crisis or jettison them in the struggle to survive?

Leaders may find it necessary to realign or redefine the organization's values and vision to make them more potent or relevant not only during times of crisis but also when everything is operating normally. Values may have to be reworded to make them stronger (an obvious example is an increased emphasis on employee safety), new values may need to be added, and obsolete values may need to be eliminated. If values that were found to be irrelevant or were ignored during the crisis are not altered or cut, they pose the risk of becoming a joke among the employees and threatening the leadership's credibility.

Because effective postcrisis leadership involves focusing on the human side of the situation, attention must also be paid to personal values. The high-pressure environment of a crisis can stress or damage relationships, and these need to be rebuilt and strengthened. Again, communication is the foundation on which the relationship restoration process is built, and establishing an atmosphere in which people feel safe talking about their feelings and in which a premium is placed on forgiveness is key.

WORKING PLANS

The final piece of the postcrisis puzzle for leaders is attending to the organization's operational needs. In many cases a significant cleanup effort is required—recovery, repair and rebuilding, and reorganizing. Human resource issues also need to be addressed; personnel voids may need to be filled by promoting current employees or hiring replacement workers.

Operational concerns after a crisis inevitably involve the financial repercussions, such as the costs of cleaning up, salvaging, rebuilding, managing public relations, and working overtime. Sometimes the potential for litigation poses the most far-reaching implications for an organization's finances—a follow-up lawsuit can place the organization in a crisis situation far worse than the one it has just endured—and leaders need to stay thoroughly apprised and attuned on the legal front.

IMAGE COUNTS

When leaders fail to handle a crisis adeptly and sensitively—and sometimes even when they do the best job possible—organizational damage, problems, and challenges will inevitably result. The organization's reputation may be hurt, stock values may plunge, key employees may leave, and lawsuits may loom.

Organizations live and die by their reputations, so it's essential that leaders develop a strategy to restore the organizational reputation after a crisis. The best way to do this is to implement a concerted public relations campaign focusing on employees, shareholders, the media, the community, and public interest groups. By reestablishing the organization's reputation, by affirming a sense of security and well-being, leaders can reduce the emotional impact of the crisis and strengthen the connection between the organization and its employees and stakeholders. If leaders can accomplish this, they will have taken a big step toward helping the organization emerge from a crisis not only intact but also with a better and more effective foundation.

Pressure Cooking: Real Leaders Thrive When the Chips Are Down

Graham Jones

The role of the leader involves several principal tasks: creating a compelling vision, coming up with a strategy to achieve that vision, and communicating the vision and strategy to the organization's people. All of this puts the leader in a highly visible position, in which expectations can create enormous pressure. In tough economic times such as the world is experiencing now, this pressure is intensified. Leaders' success in such environments depends largely on the path they choose: to be *safe* leaders or *real* leaders.

The fundamental job of a leader is to establish a clear vision for his or her people—they want to know where their leader intends to take them. But the job doesn't end there. Leaders must then formulate a strategy and plan so that their people know how the vision will be achieved and what is expected of them. Next, the vision and strategy have to be communicated to the people who are being asked to deliver it. This is where leaders must demonstrate a level of logic that is bulletproof if they are to secure their people's buy-in and engagement. In communicating the vision and strategy, leaders must also show genuine emotion, oozing a passion that will inspire everyone to follow. This whole process means that they will be highly visible, exposed, and vulnerable.

Many senior leaders are so highly visible that they sometimes feel isolated and lonely. Everyone wants to be their friend. In fact, they have so many "friends" that they are sometimes unable to identify who their true friends and allies are.

Such visibility can weigh heavily on the shoulders of leaders. The expectations their people and they themselves have can be enormous, to the extent that leaders may secretly wonder if they

are up to the task. In my work with senior executives I have had a number of them tell me, when behind closed doors, "I'm waiting to be found out," or, "I'm wondering how I got to this position; I don't feel comfortable in it."

The responsibilities and accountabilities of leaders do not, of course, cease when they have secured the buy-in of people via a compelling vision delivered with passion. The demands are incessant in the daily grind of operating in an environment where leaders are expected to be decisive, know the answers, be role models, and deliver results. Get it wrong and they can lose many of those newly acquired "friends" and "allies."

DIFFICULT TIMES

As if this routine situation does not constitute a sufficiently demanding challenge, leaders are doubly or even exponentially tested when times are tough.

Good economic climates can hide many of the flaws in corporations, and poor leadership and inept leaders often go unnoticed in such favorable times. Too often, as long as results are delivered, there are few questions asked about *how* they are delivered.

Things are very different when times are tough. Leaders have never been more highly visible than during the recent dramatic difficulties facing the business world. This has been a rollercoaster environment that has engulfed large corporations that once seemed untouchable. This is when outstanding leadership is so crucial, but it also happens to be when outstanding leadership is very difficult to deliver.

In difficult times, employees need and want to be able to trust their leaders to be open and to let the employees know how things stand. Leaders also need to recognize that an inevitable part of change and turbulent times is that many of their people will view the situation as a catastrophe and that they will need the leaders' help to deal with it. Listening to employees' concerns, showing empathy, and reminding them of successes, however small, always have to be at the forefront of a leader's mind in these circumstances. But leaders must also continue to focus on a strategy for moving forward and keeping employees focused on delivering quality service and products to customers.

SHOWING RESILIENCE

This is where having a vision for getting through the tough times is so important. Many leaders fail to understand that visions are equally as important, if not more important, during turbulent times as during more normal times. Leaders need a vision of how the organization, business unit, or team will deal with the current difficulties and emerge stronger. This type of vision is about organizational resilience, reminding people about what they are good at and what is required from them, and telling a story of how the challenges will be overcome.

The best example of this in my experience of working with leaders in tough times is Ben, the leader of a building materials company experiencing a serious downturn in a rapidly shrinking economy. In the midst of announcing job losses, Ben also spent time telling the people who remained about his vision of how the organization would emerge from the difficulties stronger than when it entered them. He reminded his people of their skills and abilities and the resilience they had shown in previous downturns. Ben talked about how people would grow and develop during the tough times ahead and how the company would retain its top talent to ensure it maintained its competitive advantage when better times returned. He told them how the company would seek and find opportunities that it would seize on because of the optimism it would carry forward. This was a great example of a vision that reflected the resilience required in tough times.

FACING A CHOICE

Of course, all this fortitude is demanded of leaders when they may be feeling pretty worried and pessimistic themselves. Clients, employees, shareholders, and the media are but a few of the stake-holders who watch leaders very carefully to see how they cope under such circumstances.

So in turbulent economic markets, even the best leaders are stretched to their limits. What has worked in the past may not work in these current difficult times. This is when the pressure cauldron that leaders find themselves in either makes or breaks them.

At times the pressure on leaders may be so great that they wonder whether it's all worth it and why they have put themselves in this situation. In fact, have you ever considered why leaders choose to be leaders? Is it about the status, package, power, and authority that come with the role? Is it the required responsibility, accountability, and vision that attract them? Or is it about the op-portunity to make a difference and have a real impact?

My experience in coaching numerous senior leaders has led me to believe that different people have different motives for being leaders. From these observations and experiences, I have identified two types of leaders: *real* leaders and *safe* leaders. This distinction has been apparent to me across all market conditions but has been particularly evident in turbulent times. Tough economic condi-tions bring an intriguing quandary for leaders. These are the times when leaders must make a choice between settling in as safe lead-ers and stepping up to be real leaders.

What are some of the key differences between safe and real leaders?

Safe leaders

- Are driven by their needs for rewards, status, and power and are therefore unwilling to put themselves on the line for fear of losing their position if they get it wrong.

- Focus on what they need to do to ensure that they conform to company practices and procedures.

- Rarely innovate or challenge orthodoxy because their focus is almost exclusively on micromanaging in the short term.

- React mainly to immediate, day-to-day, ongoing issues.
- Are fearful of making mistakes because these might affect their job security.
- Look to blame others when things go wrong.
- Claim others' successes as their own.
- View challenge as unhelpful and threatening.
- Encourage conformity to tried-and-tested methods.
- Pay lip service to change initiatives.
- Settle for good rather than pushing for great.
- Are reluctant and slow to tackle underperformance.
- Claim that they are only the messenger when it's time to communicate tough decisions.

Real leaders

- Are driven by the challenge and opportunity to put themselves out there and make a difference—this is what leadership is all about for them.
- Focus on providing a good role model for their people.
- Empower others to focus on managing the short-term challenges so that their own minds can focus more on innovating and investing in the future.
- Create a road map for the future.
- Accept that they are highly visible.
- See mistakes as a key part of their development and learning.
- Accept responsibility and accountability when things go wrong.
- Are courageous in seeking to understand the causes of failure.
- Recognize the contributions of others to successes.

- Encourage challenge and collective problem solving.
- Encourage people to challenge accepted ways of thinking and acting.
- Challenge themselves and others to raise the performance bar.
- Address underperformance when it arises.
- Make and own tough decisions.

Safe leaders exist in various guises, so different leaders will exhibit the traits in varying degrees. What is common across them is their reluctance to put themselves on the line; they have too much to lose if they get it wrong.

I worked with one safe leader whose "motive" was noticeable in his resistance to identifying a vision and a long-term strategy and plan for his organization. Instead he chose to keep himself busy by reacting to the usual day-to-day events, and that kept him off the firing line.

In another case, a business unit head clearly hid behind an overt claim that her style was to lead through consensus. This led to excessive debate and conflict among her team of opinionated, strong-willed, and competitive individuals, and so she was too slow in making the decisions that needed to be made. She was playing it safe.

Real leaders also come in different shapes and sizes. One managing director of a large distribution company was very clear about what was non-negotiable when it came to providing quality customer service. This meant introducing metrics that would highlight areas of weakness and be unpopular with some of her people because they were at risk of being exposed as underperformers. Not all members of the company's board of directors agreed with her either, but she was resolute in her rationale and the new metrics resulted in a significant improvement in customer satisfaction. Here was a real leader who was willing to challenge the status quo.

In another case I witnessed a managing director bring about a sharp increase in performance in his professional services company. The organization was already performing well, but the managing director thought this performance could still be significantly improved and that employees were not stretching themselves. He had a choice to make: he could either play it safe and oversee the continued success of the organization and enjoy his popularity when it came to bonus time, or he could challenge his people to stretch themselves and achieve their true potential. He chose to be a real leader and started to communicate his thoughts about how the future of the organization was threatened by a complacency that was becoming ever more apparent. His calls for everyone to raise the performance bar were met with derision by some of his people, but this turned out to be the foundation of the company's step up to the next performance level.

RAISING THE STAKES

The differences between real and safe leaders are particularly evident and pronounced during tough and turbulent times for organizations. Remember that what lies at the core of safe leaders is role security. These leaders value the prestige, status, power, authority, and financial package that come with leadership. There is a lot to lose for these leaders, so much so that particularly in tough times, their main focus will be staying off the firing line and becoming even more risk averse; not taking risks, to them, means ensuring no mistakes. They withdraw into a safety zone. They believe that now is the time to avoid conflict, and so it becomes too risky to challenge peers' or bosses' views. They spend less time coaching their people and more time telling their subordinates what to do and how to do it. They are careful about what they say, and they sit tight in the hope that more favorable times are just around the corner. Their focus is on cutting costs and hitting short-term targets. Tough times bring conditions in which safe leaders will not thrive. On the contrary, they will be stressed and debilitated and will eventually founder in an environment full of apparent threats to their safety.

At the other end of the continuum, real leaders are driven mainly by the challenge and the opportunity to put themselves out there, make a difference, and have a real impact. They thrive on the pressure that is the inescapable companion of tough times. This is their calling; they come to the fore and are even more highly visible. They focus on what they can control and make things happen. Real leaders make decisions and stand by them and "tell it like it is." They view tough economic climates as being times when development is most needed; these are the times to nurture and retain talent in order to gain competitive advantage in the long term.

Their skills are even more prominent as they strive to lead the organization and support their people through turbulent, sometimes catastrophic, circumstances. This is when their personal resources are so important, to the extent that they unwittingly or perhaps deliberately expose them to their people. Their resilience, optimism balanced with realism, strength of character, vast experience, care, and determination will be very evident. But so too will the fact that they are human beings like everyone else. They also have doubts and worries, and believe that there is no point in hiding them. Real leaders are authentic, and their impact in organizations is much more a function of *how they are* than *what they do*.

CORE QUALITIES

Real leaders hold the key to the future health of all organizations. Yet too often organizations allow safe leaders to perpetuate the status quo and hinder progress and innovation. What lies at the core of this issue is that people continue to get promoted to leadership positions mostly because they are good at what they do. But leadership is not about being a good accountant, engineer, lawyer, mathematician, investment banker, or the like. Instead, it is about two core qualities:

1. The motivation to be a real leader and to accept everything that comes with that role, including
   - Being held accountable when things go wrong
   - Having the confidence to let go
   - Being willing to make mistakes
   - Having the courage to make and own tough decisions
   - Having the conviction to do the right thing
   - Focusing on creating a road map for the future
   - Taking on the responsibility to drive change
   - Being comfortable with the visibility of being a good role model
   - Striving for continual personal growth and learning
2. The capacity to thrive on pressure; this requires
   - Remaining in control when the pressure is at its most ferocious
   - Building a resilient self-belief
   - Maintaining motivation when things are tough
   - Staying focused on the things that matter
   - Harnessing thoughts and feelings so they remain positive
   - Turning threats into opportunities
   - Bouncing back from setbacks
   - Learning from mistakes
   - Establishing a good work-life balance

WHAT IT MEANS

The implications for organizations address three levels. First, real leadership should form the core focus of leadership development programs aimed at ensuring the future health of the organization.

Second, an organization should emphasize mind-set as well as competencies when assessing leadership potential. Finally, the ability to thrive on pressure can be developed. Because pressure is an inevitable and inescapable component of leadership, organizations need to provide these development opportunities for their leaders.

The Narrative Lens and Organizational Change

Nick Nissley and Stedman Graham

What do a CEO and a six-year-old child grieving over the death of her pet dog have in common? More than you might think. Recently a friend told us a story about her daughter, who after the death of the family's chocolate Labrador said, "I wish we could just give Woody a pill and make him a puppy again." It reminded us that when people's health fails them, they often seek *prescriptions*. Our friend's daughter was hoping for a drug remedy to restore her dog's health and vitality.

Later that evening we attended a client engagement in San Diego, where we listened to the organization's CEO speak to more than a hundred shareholders, telling them the story of the organization he founded. He proudly talked about the company's founding and its history of winning. But he also painted an honest picture of a less-than optimistic market outlook and the complex challenges and risks the company was facing. He said that strategies that had worked for the company in the past would no longer help it navigate through future challenges. He described how the company would be forced to shift gears. He confidently told the shareholders that a new strategic plan had been drawn up at the company's recent leadership retreat and that his management team was beginning to deliver on it.

After the CEO finished speaking, we reflected on his speech. His approach sounded quite similar to approaches detailed in many other executives' speeches to shareholders we had heard over the past few years.

The next day we continued to reflect on the similarity of the CEO's speech to many we had heard before. At the same time, our friend's story of her daughter's response to the death of the family dog—her desire for a prescription to make everything right—was percolating in our minds. We came to appreciate both stories through the lens of narrative. The CEO was telling his shareholders a story—actually two stories: one a proud story of organizational health and the other, like the story of Woody, a story of demise and the desire to restore good health. It was as if the CEO had to let go of one script and embrace another—a new strategic plan for his team to enact.

In the months following our experience in San Diego, we came to more fully appreciate the power of the narrative lens. The business world in recent years has shown increasing interest in the narrative lens and more specifically in the relationship between leadership storytelling and organizational change. Consider some of the recently published books that address the power of leadership storytelling: *The Power of Story: Rewrite Your Destiny in Business and in Life*, by Jim Loehr (Free Press, 2007); *Whoever Tells the Best Story Wins: How to Use Your Own Stories to Communicate with Power and Impact*, by Annette Simmons (AMACOM, 2007); and *The Leader's Guide to Storytelling: Mastering the Art and Discipline of Business Narrative*, by Stephen Denning (Jossey-Bass, 2005). It was becoming clearer to us: leaders must cultivate their awareness of the stories they are a part of, and they must be able to transform those stories when old stories no longer serve their organizations. However, as our own curiosity revealed, leaders and leadership development practitioners know relatively little about how to engage in this process.

REWRITING DESTINIES

In Loehr's *The Power of Story*, he suggests that leaders may face a time when they must rewrite their destinies. He asserts that because leaders' destinies follow their stories, it's imperative that they do everything in their power to get their stories right. He says leaders may have to consider editing a dysfunctional story and asking themselves the question, "In which important areas of my life is it clear that I cannot achieve my goals with the story I've got?"

"That's it," we thought. Our experience in San Diego, which was being played out similarly in corporate boardrooms across the country, was being described by Loehr. Although Loehr is discussing something that occurs at an individual level—rewriting personal stories—leaders can ask the question he suggests not just about their own goals but also about organizational goals: "Why can we not achieve our company's goals with the story we have?" This question, framed by the narrative lens, affords leaders a new perspective.

Here's where theory—narrative theory—can help leaders better understand how they can effect change. *Narratives* allow leaders to prepare for and guide their actions. Narratives, or stories, are composed of bits we refer to as *scripts*. Scripting produces an ordered set of expectations about what will happen next; it's a means by which one moves a story forward. Thus, when leaders need to find new stories, new ways forward, they must articulate new scripts. We realized that the process movie directors and screenwriters use to keep audiences engaged may also, often unconsciously, be used by leaders in the workplace.

We call this process of leaders finding new stories when old ones no longer serve their needs *rescription*. It is a powerful tool for guiding actions when change is needed. As executive coaches, we are finding ourselves being called on by leaders to help them find the tools to *right* their organizations by *rewriting* the stories that are no longer effectively serving their organizations. Leaders are asking themselves, "Can we achieve our goals with the story we have?" Honest answers to this question are often leading to the leadership actions we refer to as rescription.

SHIFTING GEARS

Rescription is perhaps nowhere more visible than in the case of the U.S. Big Three automakers—Chrysler, Ford, and General Motors. On the brink of collapse, these automakers, in late December 2008, received up to $17.4 billion in emergency loans, with the caveat that they restructure and demonstrate their viability by the end of March 2009. The automakers were forced to retool and shift gears. They could no longer rely on the trucks and sport-utility vehicles that in the past provided a large portion of their revenue. A new story line emerged in Detroit. The new script reflected a radical rethinking and change: shifting production from trucks and SUVs to small, fuel-efficient passenger cars.

For example, President and CEO Alan Mulally continues to lead the rescription at Ford, which had a loss of $15.3 billion in 2006–2007. At the heart of Ford's strategy was a plant retooling that would allow the company to build its next generation of passenger cars on a common platform, resulting in significant savings in production costs. Mulally is using the power of story—rescripting the company's strategy—to effect change at Ford.

THREE-STEP PROCESS

Unlike our friend's daughter who was grieving over the death of her pet dog, executives cannot rely on a childlike naiveté and simply wish for healthful rejuvenation. Rescription is the organizational antidote that's needed when a company can no longer achieve its goals with its existing story. Rescriptions are similar to physicians' prescriptions that restore good health to ailing individuals. The organizational physician is the company's leader, who must courageously and accurately prescribe a new way of doing business—as Ford's Mulally is doing by rescripting the company from one focused on making trucks and SUVs to one focused on manufacturing efficient and economical cars.

How can leaders undertake the process of rescription? From our observations, we have devised a three-step process for rescription: titling the present script, founding the future script, and actualizing the new script.

Titling the Present Script

First, leaders must face the truth and honestly identify the present scripts that are being enacted. Many leaders struggle to accurately diagnose their current challenge. Effective leaders must not only diagnose the challenge but also communicate it in such a way that everyone in the organization believes the leader and commits to the interpretation. The most effective leaders are able to title the story that's being played out, affording others in the organization an opportunity to easily grasp the challenge. Ford's Mulally honestly identified the debilitating, truck-and-SUV-centric script of the auto manufacturer. To armchair analysts this may seem to have been a simple step. However, as all of Detroit knows, breaking from what worked in the past is more difficult than it appears. In many ways, leaders need to articulate what's *stuck*. Good leaders, like good writers, identify a future turning point and what needs to become *unstuck*. Turning points are not always obvious— many are subtle and recognizable only in hindsight.

Founding the Future Script

Once leaders have confronted and identified the dysfunctional present script—in which the company is stuck—they must even more courageously ask what's needed when the company can no longer achieve its goals with the story it has. By asking what's needed, leaders open the door to considering an alternative script and founding a future narrative that will identify what's needed to become unstuck. When Mulally asked the "what's needed" question, he accessed the automaker's engineering intellectual capital. The organizational response to his questioning was the global-platform concept. Ford realized that to achieve significant savings in production costs, it needed a common base on which to build its next generation of passenger cars.

Actualizing the New Script

The third and final step is to take the answer to the "what's needed" question and begin to act on it. Writers refer to this step as *actualizing the narrative* or *enactment*. If action doesn't transpire, the new story remains an unrealized dream. Mulally initiated this step when he traveled to Wall Street to meet with analysts and

Helping Leaders See New Possibilities

Recently, Nick Nissley conducted a rescription workshop in the University of Oxford's strategic leadership executive education program. As a former executive, program director Marshall Young is astutely aware that executives often become stuck in dysfunctional story lines and find themselves repeating scripts that don't yield the desired results. He also understands the value of the narrative lens as a tool for helping executives see new possibilities when they're stuck.

So Young encouraged Nissley to develop an experiential learning opportunity that would offer the participants a practical tool to develop new scripts that would allow them to move their stories forward.

Nissley used CCL's Visual Explorer tool to aid the rescription exercise. Visual Explorer enables imagination and encourages dialogue through the use of visual imagery. The tool comprises more than a hundred diverse images that help people visualize their challenges and imagine new possibilities.

Participants were first asked to consider a challenge they were facing—where they felt they were stuck. They then found an image from Visual Explorer that spoke to them, helping them visually explain the challenge they were dealing with. Then they found a partner to begin a dialogue with about the challenge, using the Visual Explorer image to help describe the challenge. The partners were engaging in the first step of the rescription process—titling the present script. Second, the partners were asked to find another Visual Explorer image that suggested a way out—a possibility for getting unstuck. This simple technique helped the participants access their imaginations and begin visualizing a future script. Again the partners engaged in a dialogue mediated by their Visual Explorer images. What they found was that the images and dialogue offered insights and a more expansive vocabulary in order to surface a future script that would enable them to become unstuck. This is the second step in the rescription process—founding the future script. Finally, the participants needed to consider the process of enactment—actualizing the new script. In this phase Nissley played a greater coaching role, asking the participants what was needed for them to enact the third and final stage of the rescription process—letting go of the old script and embracing the new one.

At the end of the workshop, one participant commented: "I knew I was stuck, but I didn't know how to get unstuck. The Visual Explorer images allowed me to see new possibilities—I was literally able to see a new script emerge as my partner and I dialogued about my challenge." To be sure, the use of Visual Explorer isn't a sort of tarot card exercise in which executives have their futures read. Rather it is a blending of narrative therapy-like techniques with creative visualization techniques that enables leadership storytelling. It is a practical tool for helping leaders when they are stuck and need a new script that allows them to move their stories forward.

the news media and begin telling the new story, the rescription for Ford's future good health. However, there is much more to be done. The true measure of a successful rescription is the whole-hearted acceptance of the executive's compelling new narrative by those in the organization and their subsequent adoption of effective actions toward the desired outcome.

TIME FOR A CHANGE

As we have noted, leaders, leadership development practitioners, and executive coaches have become increasingly aware in recent years of the importance of narrative competence to the success of leaders. This is evidenced by the growing number of books, course offerings in MBA programs, and executive development programs that delve into this subject. However, little insight as yet exists into *how* leaders are engaging story as a means to lead more effectively, and especially into *how* a narrative lens might afford a new perspective on leading through times of change.

Our observation of the rescription process has led us to ponder as we look through the narrative lens, seeking new perspectives on leadership, how might playwrights, theater directors, screenwriters, and others involved in the narrative arts offer insights into how to lead and effect change in organizations?

We ask you to consider this: Is your organization's dominant story allowing the organization to achieve its goals? Or is it time to rewrite your organization's story? If an organization and its leaders can no longer achieve their goals with the story they have, it's time for a leadership rescription.

A Tale of Three Countries Offers Valuable Knowledge

Yi Zhang

Over the past thirty years much research has been conducted in the United States and Europe on the experiences that help leaders learn, grow, and change. Until recently, however, little such research has been conducted in Asia. But that is gradually changing. A comparison of studies by CCL and others on organizational changes and how they can be leveraged to accelerate leadership development—conducted in the United States, India, and more recently, China—offers new insights into how the lessons leaders learn through organizational changes vary among the respective countries. It also reveals significant implications for practitioners striving to understand and analyze the relationship between organizational changes and leadership development.

Organizational changes—which may include hierarchical shifts, new projects, and variations in performance—are increasingly prevalent in India and China as a result of the dynamic economic developments in those two nations. After such organizational changes, leaders typically have a better understanding of themselves and of ways to manage change and deal with crises. Organizational changes tend to force leaders to move from inertia into a transitional state. If they are able to adapt and learn, they are likely to succeed; if not, they may be derailed—held in place, demoted, or even fired.

SCOPE AND PACE

The research done in China involved in-depth interviews conducted with more than fifty senior Chinese managers from large companies in a variety of industries. The interviews focused on this question: "Which three major experiences in your work or personal lives were key to your development, and what have you learned from these events?"

The researchers then analyzed the organizational changes reported in the interviews. The responses were organized first into *thought units*. For example, one manager who worked on restructuring his organization's entire sales system succeeded in producing a substantial profit for the company; he learned from this and afterward changed both his managerial practices and his views and perspectives.

In the second phase all the thought units were organized into *emergent categories*—for example, being involved in a merger or acquisition; experiencing a new or different organizational culture, system, or process; getting an opportunity to develop a new product or service or start a unit, plant, or line of business from scratch; and turning around a failing business operation.

In the third phase the categories were grouped under three themes in organizational change: *strategic and structural changes, new initiatives*, and *fix-it events*. In the model of organizational change developed by University of Alberta business professors Royston Greenwood and C. R. Hinings, change has two dimensions: *scope* and *pace*. The pace of change can be either *revolutional* or *evolutional*. Revolutional change often replaces an old structure, strategy, or program with a new one. Organizations initiate revolutional changes in multiple domains, including technology, structure, and top management, with a view to improving performance and enhancing adaptability. Evolutional change is often perceived as a small adaptation and as part of ongoing modifications in organizational processes and practices.

Strategic and structural changes occur at the organizational level. Examples from the research in China are being involved in a merger or acquisition; downsizing; being part of an organization that expands in any form; experiencing new or different organizational cultures, systems, or processes; a regulatory review; a major implementation of significant systems or process changes; and installing new systems that managers are unfamiliar with. These can be considered large-scope, revolutional changes.

New initiatives involve building something from nothing. Managers get the opportunity to develop a new product or service or start a unit, plant, or line of business from scratch; introduce new technology; or expand a market to a new region of the country or to another country, at times conceptualizing it, setting it up, and growing it. These changes can be viewed as small-scope revolutional changes.

Fix-it events involve turning around a failing business operation (for example, one with low sales or negative growth), taking it from incurring losses or barely breaking even to being profitable. The Chinese managers described serious problems that led to poor business performance, such as resistant attitudes, people and morale issues, a lack of efficient systems and processes, and malfunctioning operational processes that significantly hindered productivity. A fix-it event usually leads to a positive outcome, but occasionally the outcome is initially seen as negative, as in the case of a branch closing, for example. These changes can be viewed as small-scope evolutional changes.

DIFFERENT TRENDS

Although these three themes emerged in the research in all three countries, the nature of the events and the lessons learned varied among the countries. Therefore the effects of the pace and the scope of organizational changes on the development of managers may be different. The China study identified developmental experiences among managers similar to those found in a recent study of CEOs in the United States. However, some trends found in the China and India studies were different from those found in the U.S. research.

• Strategic and structural changes contributed greatly to Chinese and U.S. managers' learning but not much to Indian managers' development. Country reforms in China influenced organizational reforms and therefore the experiences and learning of Chinese managers from these changes. Chinese organizational changes came mostly from structural shifts and acquisitions, whereas U.S. organizational changes were more diverse.

• New initiative changes greatly influenced Chinese and Indian managers' growth but did not much influence U.S. managers' growth; such changes made a big impression on Indian and Chinese managers, but only around 10 percent of U.S. managers considered them important events. This result may mean that U.S. managers do not have many new initiatives in their organizations, which tend to be longer established than Chinese and Indian organizations, or it may mean that the U.S. managers had had so many such experiences that they saw them as commonplace.

• Fix-it changes were considered important by managers from all three countries; they made up about one-third of the organizational changes that managers cited as impressive. One such change, described as important by a Chinese manager, was that after fixing a problem, he and his team significantly increased the amount of insurance sold by his company. An Indian manager described a major fix-it change this way: "Nothing was right, the team was not good enough, the portfolio was bad, market conditions had deteriorated after September eleventh and the bursting of the Internet bubble, the company had no money, and the expectations were huge. I had to create a new charter from nothing." Despite the odds he turned the company around and learned from the experience.

The types of lessons that managers learned from changes differed among the countries. U.S. and Chinese managers learned more about managerial and technical skills, whereas Indian managers learned more about themselves.

Chinese managers learned how to develop managerial skills, value customer orientation, reduce risk, manage teams, and communicate. U.S. managers learned how to manage change and crisis, manage subordinates, develop strategic and technical skills, and behave with integrity. Indian managers learned how to build confidence, innovate and create, strengthen self-awareness, develop technical skills, gain influence, and focus on customer orientation.

Although the data collection is not complete, the initial findings could offer a new explanation for the varied results that managers in the different countries experience from organizational changes.

With the increase in global competitiveness, today's organizations experience constant change and typically are stable only for short periods of time between changes. Organizational changes represent both opportunities and threats for managers. However, research findings such as these may help managers take advantage of change opportunities and be better prepared for change. Organizations may become more cognizant of the changes that influence managers' development most and what managers can learn from these changes. This knowledge may help organizations both select and develop managers. Organizations may be able to apply the lessons learned by currently successful top executives as assessment dimensions when developing high-potential managers into future effective top executives. And they may be able to use this knowledge to select managers who have had the relevant experiences and learned the pertinent lessons that will enable them to lead future changes.

A Kinder, Gentler, and Better Way to Downsize

Nick Yacabucci

When an organization decides, for whatever reason, that it has to cut its workforce, the standard practice is to bring in an outplacement firm to help with the painful and legally hazardous task of moving people out. Once people are notified that they will be leaving the organization, a representative of the outplacement firm is available to help them understand the situation. After the employees depart, they can use the outplacement firm for assistance in putting together résumés and resources and, for a limited time, looking for another job.

The other challenges that organizations face during these difficult transitions—such as redefining job positions and deciding who will fill them—are handled separately. In my view, this classical approach to downsizing is needlessly destructive—a classic case of too little, too late. It yields stressed-out survivors who face more work and fewer resources and former employees who feel abandoned. Performance decreases, and the reputation of the organization suffers.

I believe that organizations can avoid the destructiveness of downsizing while accomplishing the objectives that prompted the reduction and even doing some good in the process. The key is to address as early as possible both the career issues of all employees and the organization's transitional challenges.

NAVIGATING CHANGE

There is no doubt that it is a good idea for organizations to bring in people who can help with the challenges involved in downsizing. But instead of hiring outplacement counselors, a better approach is to engage *navigational coaches*—professionals who are expert both in helping people make good choices about their work lives and in helping organizations manage enterprise-wide transitions. These coaches can help plan and implement an integrated approach to transition.

Ideally, navigational coaches should be brought in to help management once it has realized that a transition must occur but before it has determined what to do and how to do it. The coaches can attend planning meetings; advise management on setting up revised organizational objectives, strategies, and structures; and most important, assist in devising effective processes for consolidating and re-staffing the organization after the downsizing.

At the same time, navigational coaches can work with employees to help them understand their professional and personal strengths, weaknesses, and goals. They can act as catalysts for connecting employees to their careers. As Edgar H. Schein, a professor emeritus at the MIT Sloan School of Management, has written about uncovering one's *career anchor*, "regardless of your present job, your future decisions will be easier and more valid if you have a clear understanding of your own orientation toward work, your motives, your values, and your self-perceived talents."

Navigational coaches can thus help an organization do more than just let people go. For instance, they can help in seeding the revised organization with the best talent. As management evaluates employees for re-staffing, basing its evaluations on revised job and leadership competencies, people can be placed into one of three categories: A for the best talent, B for solid performers, and C for employees with the lowest job and leadership competency scores. Concurrently, employees can gain a better understanding of their own contributions to the organization. With this ranking system and improved employee understanding, the organization can deal more effectively with three fundamental issues:

Newly created positions. Downsizing typically requires the organization to establish new positions to handle redistributed work and to match employees' competencies to the new job requirements. The revised organization needs to ask, What types of knowledge, skills, and abilities are required in these positions to accomplish the organization's objectives? Place only A players in the newly created jobs.

Existing positions in the revised organization. Many positions will stay the same. Keep the same employees in those jobs if they are A players. If they are not, keep or place B players in those jobs and develop them quickly to A level.

Separations. When there is a downsizing, all employees need to consider the possibility of leaving the organization, whether by voluntary separation, involuntary separation, early retirement, or normal retirement. During the transition, coaches can encourage employees to determine their future based on their career options and the feedback they receive from the leadership team and the evaluation scores.

This career management process can help the leadership team differentiate long-term A players—people who are definitely committed to staying with and rebuilding the organization—from short-term A players—people who are looking to move on. And it provides this information much earlier than many other career management processes. Surprisingly, if offered a separation option, some A employees may decide to leave the organization—and the organization may be better off if they do, especially if they are not long-term players.

An early differentiation of long-and short-term A players is a form of risk management for the organization. For instance, as with the evaluation of any other asset, there are two key questions the organization can ask:

- What is the long-term risk associated with the investment in each employee?
- What is the long-term risk of not investing in all employees by providing them with the appropriate training and development, equipment, technology, and so on?

The answers can be quantified and used in combination with other risk-assessment criteria to improve the effectiveness of long-term workforce planning, succession planning, and investment decisions.

Those employees who are chosen for or who choose separation should be handled much differently from the way employees are typically treated during outplacement. There should be a transition period, ideally ninety days, during which they continue to receive career coaching, collaborating with their coaches to create career campaigns that provide realistic plans for pursuing situations outside the organization. This collaboration should be confidential and fully supported by the leadership team.

The departing employees should be coached through a career campaign that offers real help in obtaining another job— unless of course the person has chosen the option of full retirement. The coaches open up their networks of contacts, ask other coaches to open up their networks, and encourage the employees to do the same, thus creating a database of opportunities for face-to-face interviews.

MAKING IT WORK

The navigational coaching process should also have the following characteristics:

The coach should go to the departing employee, meeting him or her in convenient locations. Visiting an outplacement office can be unsettling or even humiliating—and employees seldom visit such offices after the first month or so. (Research shows that once a person has a good résumé, cover letter, networking list, and list of targeted organizations, he or she needs face-to-face contacts to get a job.)

The departing employee should be coached through a complete process of planning, perspective taking, preparation, practice, and referrals. Clearly, this is much more than the standard outplacement effort, which frequently amounts to a couple of hours of providing information on severance and benefits, a couple of hours of polishing the résumé, and an hour or so on the importance of networking—all provided over a period of weeks, at the end of which severance pay is often about to run out. Also, to make this fuller process work, the coach must provide value to the prospective new employer by referring only highly qualified people and by verifying their backgrounds.

The process should continue until the departing employee has found a new job. Providing just a couple of months of help will not benefit most people. In general, it takes a month of searching for every $10,000 of salary a person is seeking.

Throughout, the objective is to place the separated employees in positions with new organizations or in self-employment situations as soon as possible. This approach can provide numerous benefits:

- The departing employees are not subjected to organizational humiliation and they leave with greater dignity.

- The retained employees see this process as a more civilized transition and are likely to use it themselves if they become leaders.

- The organization may realize lower overall transition costs: smaller severance payments, lower legal fees because fewer separation agreements have to be developed, and so on.

A navigational career management process can also help organizations with other challenging transitions—for instance, making a choice at the crossroads of whether to continue to invest in existing employees through training and development or whether to go out and buy the needed talent in the marketplace.

Through the navigational career management process, employees can build their careers by working with the leadership team and the coaches to consider development alternatives inside or outside the organization. When the alternatives are identified, the employees and the organization are better equipped to manage transitions.

Another transition challenge is the employee who is eligible for early or regular retirement. Even at normal retirement age, many people are ready for a change but not for full retirement. How do these employees fit into this career coaching and transition process? The same way as any other employee looking for his or her next job.

The time is now for organizational leaders to set a vision that contains a career management process enabling all employees to be successful. Leaders are seeing how important career-oriented questions are to developing a clear vision and a more adaptable organization: What core and job competencies are required? What applications of those competencies benchmark employees as A players now and in the future? Can the organization win without A players in pivotal jobs?

By engaging specially trained career coaches to work with management and employees from planning all the way through transition, a downsizing organization can experience improved morale and a speedier recovery time, resulting in higher productivity and decreased costs. And the people who leave the organization can be helped to continue, and perhaps even advance, their productive working lives.

ABOUT THE CONTRIBUTORS

Kerry A. Bunker is founder and president of Mangrove Leadership Solutions, an executive development firm. He is also founding partner of MEM Partners (Making Experience Matter). Previously he was a senior fellow and manager of the Awareness Program for Executive Excellence at CCL.

Allan Calarco is a senior faculty member at CCL.

Keir Carroll, a former CCL faculty member, is founder and head of Keir Carroll & Associates, which specializes in designing and delivering workshops that boost leadership and communication skills throughout organizations.

Robert A. Goldberg is an adjunct with and a former program manager at CCL. He is a principal of Organization Insight, a North Carolina–based consulting firm specializing in change management and executive team development.

Paige Graham is a core faculty member in the School of Organizational Leadership at University of the Rockies and president of Graham Consulting Group. She was an intern at CCL in 2002.

Stedman Graham is chairman and CEO of S. Graham & Associates, a management and marketing consulting company specializing in the corporate and educational markets.

Joan Gurvis is managing director of CCL's Colorado Springs campus.

Graham Jones is cofounder of Lane4 Management Group and director of its practice in the United States. Lane4 is a performance development consultancy that specializes in creating high-performance environments in organizations.

Stu Kantor is an executive coach, business consultant, and president of Kantor Consulting Associates, an executive development firm.

Gene Klann is owner of Leading With Character, a professional training and coaching firm. Previously he was a senior faculty member at CCL after a twenty-five-year career in the U.S. Army.

Kathy E. Kram is a professor of organizational behavior and the Shipley Professor in Management at the Boston University School of Management.

Richard Lepsinger is president of OnPoint Consulting, an organizational and leadership development firm.

Christopher Musselwhite is president and CEO of Discovery Learning, which specializes in executive education and organizational leadership development.

Nick Nissley is dean of Cincinnati State Technical and Community College's Business Technologies Division.

Susan S. Rice is a resource associate in program support at CCL.

Fabio Sala is director of organization effectiveness and development at EMC^2 Corporation, a provider of information infrastructure technology and solutions.

Michael Wakefield is president of Xander Inc., a consultancy specializing in the practical application of psychology to leadership and performance enhancement. He is also a principal with Amazon's Global Leadership Development group. Previously he was manager of trainer development at CCL, where he also designed and delivered customized, client-specific programs.

Meena S. Wilson is a senior enterprise associate at CCL, currently on assignment at CCL's campus in Jamshedpur, India.

Nick Yacabucci is CEO and managing partner of Nick Yacabucci and Associates, a compensation-consulting firm.

Gary Yukl is a professor of management at the University at Albany, State University of New York.

Yi Zhang is an associate professor of international human resource management at EMLYON Business School. Previously she was a senior research associate at CCL's Singapore campus.

Ordering Information

To get more information, to order other CCL Press publications, or to find out about bulk-order discounts, please contact us by phone at 336-545-2810 or visit our online bookstore at www.ccl.org/publications.

CPSIA information can be obtained at www.ICGtesting.com
Printed in the USA
BVOW08s1942020813

327579BV00005B/10/P

9 781604 911206